# Great Lessons in Project Management

# Great Lessons in Project Management

David Pratt, PMP

**MANAGEMENT**CONCEPTS PRESS

**MANAGEMENT**CONCEPTS PRESS
8230 Leesburg Pike, Suite 800
Tysons Corner, VA 22182
(703) 790-9595
Fax: (703) 790-1371
www.managementconcepts.com

Copyright © 2015 by Management Concepts, Inc.

All rights reserved. No part of this book may be reproduced or utilized in any form or by any means, electronic or mechanical, including photocopying, recording, or by an information storage and retrieval system, without permission in writing from the publisher, except for brief quotations in review articles.

Printed in the United States of America

Library of Congress Control Number: 2014950846

ISBN 978-1-56726-472-2
eISBN 978-1-56726-473-9

# About the Author

**David Pratt**, PMP, is a certified Project Management Professional with more than 20 years of experience in managing projects of all types and sizes. He has managed projects in both the public and private sectors in a wide variety of industries, as well as in non-profit organizations and service clubs. He is the author of *The IT Project Management Answer Book* and *Pragmatic Project Management: Five Scalable Steps to Success* as well as two novels.

A retired military officer and hospital administrator, Dave currently owns DHP Project Services, LLC. He has taught marketing, health services management, and project management at the undergraduate and graduate student levels in the United States and China. He currently teaches project management at South Puget Sound Community College in Lacey, Washington, where he led the curriculum design effort for the Project Management Certificate program.

Dave frequently speaks at conferences on topics including project management, change management, leadership, innovation, and motivation. He is a member of numerous service and professional groups, including the Project Management Institute, Lions Clubs International, World Taekwondo Federation, U.S. A. Taekwondo Association, and the Military Officers Association of America.

# About the Contributors

**Glenn Briskin,** PMP, is a project manager and consultant with more than 25 years of experience managing IT projects for public and private sector clients. He is currently the manager of IT planning and project management for the Washington State Patrol. Glenn has worked as a public sector IT manager directing projects and procuring services, a partner with a large systems integrator selling and delivering projects, and an independent consultant. He is a founding member of the Olympia, Washington, PMI chapter, an active member of the local Information Processing Managers Association, a board member of the Capital City Marathon Association, an Air Force veteran, and a U.S. Sailing certified windsurfing instructor. He writes a project management blog at www.OtherSideOfRisk.com.

**Gary Hudson,** PMP, is a professional project manager and business analyst with over 20 years of experience. His work career spans the public and private sectors, working both in staff positions and as a professional consultant. He typically works with clients to capture business requirements, conduct options analysis, develop and support the procurement process, and then select and install a solution to meet the requirements. Gary works with local professional organizations and is currently president of the Olympia, Washington, PMI chapter.

**Deborah Spaulding,** PMP, is a project management consultant with over 20 years of experience in public and private sector IT projects. Debbie created and served as the director of a project management office that achieved pivotal results in an organization new to project management. She has also managed software development departments and is a project management instructor.

# Contents

**Preface** .................................................................. xi

**Acknowledgments** ................................................. xiii

**Chapter 1** – SCOPE MANAGEMENT: If You Can See It, We Can Build It ................................................................ 1

**Chapter 2** – MANAGEMENT AND CONTROL: Can You Prove Your Project's Status? ...................................... 9

**Chapter 3** – PROJECT TEAM MANAGEMENT: Roles and Responsibilities Are Critical .................................. 17

**Chapter 4** – STAKEHOLDER MANAGEMENT: Consensus Is the Path to Success ................................................ 31

**Chapter 5** – PROJECT INITIATION: Get Your Project Off to a Good Start ........................................................ 43

**Chapter 6** – COMMUNICATIONS MANAGEMENT: Don't Let Tech-Speak Threaten Your Project ..................... 47

**Chapter 7** – QUALITY MANAGEMENT: Make Quality Your Priority .................................................................... 53

**Chapter 8** – TIME MANAGEMENT: Schedules Are Guides for Those Who Do the Work .................................... 61

**Chapter 9** – HUMAN RESOURCE MANAGEMENT: Build a Realistic Project Team ............................................. 67

**Chapter 10** – COST MANAGEMENT: Never Lose Track of the Money .................................................................... 77

**Chapter 11** – PROJECT GOVERNANCE: Organizational Support Is a Key Success Factor ........................................... 83

**Chapter 12** – PROJECT INITIATION: The Charter Is the First, Best Tool for Project Clarity ....................................... 89

**Chapter 13** – PROCUREMENT MANAGEMENT: Take the Time Necessary to Ensure Project Success ........................... 97

**Chapter 14** – PROJECT PLANNING: Those Who Do, Should Plan .................................................................... 103

**Chapter 15** – RISK MANAGEMENT: Even the Best Planning Does Not Eliminate Risk ...................................... 111

**Chapter 16** – RISK MANAGEMENT: Always Follow Up On Your Plans ................................................................ 117

**Chapter 17** – PROJECT EXECUTION: Sometimes the Napkin Approach Works .................................................. 125

**Chapter 18** – HUMAN RESOURCE MANAGEMENT: Know Your Team ................................................................... 129

**Chapter 19** – PROJECT MANAGEMENT INTEGRATION: Solution Complexity Is Seldom the Issue .......................... 137

# Preface

Projects fail at an alarming rate, whether they are information technology, training, construction, or policy development projects. No matter the focus, each year we experience an abundance of challenged projects that either require superhuman effort to resuscitate or die an untimely death.

A library of lessons learned from troubled projects—and from projects that went well—would go a long way toward enabling us to achieve more success with our own projects. Imagine a collection of stories that describe the events surrounding a particular challenge a project manager faced or a tool that another used effectively. It would be a virtual treasure trove of experiences that project managers of all types of projects could draw on to validate their own good practices and to avoid the pitfalls experienced by others.

*Great Lessons Learned in Project Management* is a first attempt to gather lessons learned from projects over several decades. Most of the stories in this book relate my own experiences working as a project manager or providing external quality assurance services for projects that were not directly under my control.

Over the past 10 years, my career efforts have been focused on resurrecting damaged or failing projects, either through my own efforts as a project manager or by providing oversight and mentoring to others managing projects. This book describes many of those efforts, all of which ended successfully. My hope is that readers will benefit from the lessons learned and thereby avoid some of the stumbling points and pitfalls so many have encountered on their projects. If it saves one project, the time it took me to write this book will have been worth the investment.

Three of the lessons-learned stories in this book were contributed by other project management professionals. Their insights offer a perspective different from my own. I have known each of the contributors for many years and can attest to their professionalism and expertise; they are seasoned project managers who understand and appreciate tried-and-true project management practices.

My vision for this book is that it will grow over the years through contributions from other project management professionals who provide their own perspectives on their project management experiences and the lessons they learned along the way. To that end, I invite anyone interested to submit well-crafted, timely lessons-learned stories in the full context of their unique situations. Perhaps this book can become a living, growing document that will provide value over many years for project managers in all areas of endeavor.

As we manage projects that provide necessary, unique products, services, and results to those we serve, I hope you will benefit from the stories and experiences captured in this book. Consider the lessons learned by those who have gone before you and recognize your own experiences as lessons learned. Then pay your experiences forward to those who might benefit from your hard-earned insights. Our discipline needs you and all that you can do to improve the services we deliver to our employers and clients.

*—Dave Pratt, PMP*
*Dave.DHP@comcast.net*

# Acknowledgments

This book would not have been possible without the suggestions and advice provided by numerous individuals. First and foremost among those is my wife who, after more than a year of my having abandoned a craft and avocation I care about deeply, asked, "Why haven't you written for so long?" Without a good reason why not, and given the frequent but friendly reminders of this book's due date from my kind and understanding publisher, I sat down and finished this book.

Second are the three project management professionals with whom I have worked in various capacities over the years who submitted chapters for this book: Debbie Spaulding, Glenn Briskin, and Gary Hudson. They are consummate professionals and good friends, and they have many stories to share. I hope that they and others like them will see the value in sharing their stories so others might learn from their experiences.

I must also thank the project management and business professionals who, through our many discussions and collaborations, have contributed to my own library of lessons learned. These include Gil Dean, PMP, Dalene Sprick, Sharon Sikes, PMP, Jennifer Carter, Noel Rubadue, Cal Brodie, Kim Brodie, Jim Anderson, Tom Wallace, Heather Anderson, Eric Vonderscheer, Mark Vetsch, Shaun Berry, Kent Meisner, and Bob Schwent.

Without a doubt, I also must thank the many students I have instructed over the years in the project management certificate program at South Puget Sound Community College and the other colleges and universities where I have taught. Their many stories, challenging questions, and insights continue to help evolve and expand my own skills.

Finally, as always, I offer my considerable thanks to my publisher, Myra Strauss, who has seen me through two previous project management books, several major life changes, and bouts of absentmindedness, and has gently kept me leaning forward toward the completion of this manuscript. Thanks, Myra. You and the crew at Management Concepts are the best. You have been great friends and allies through the several-year journey that has been the crafting of this book.

And to you, the reader, I also offer my thanks. You might be a project manager, a member of a project team, a project sponsor, or someone considering the field of project management. All I can say to you is that we need you. The failure rate of projects remains way too high across all industries. Simply by picking up this book to thumb through its pages or read its contents, you have indicated your motivation to learn, grow, and succeed.

There are too many in our field who call themselves project managers yet do not have the training or seek the knowledge to provide the highest quality service to their employers and clients. By looking beyond your current level of skill and understanding and seeking the experiences of others, you have signaled your intent to improve your capabilities and to become someone who has the background, experience, training, and information to do the job well.

This book is only one step in that direction, but just the same: Nice going, and Godspeed.

# SCOPE MANAGEMENT    1

## If You Can See It, We Can Build It

There's a saying in project management that goes something like this: "If you can see it, we can build it. But if you can't see it, we're not going anywhere." Never was this more evident than in the case of a project to replace a hunting and fishing license sales system for a large state agency.

The agency derived much of its $350 million annual revenue from the sale of hunting and fishing licenses to the public. Its old system was scheduled for retirement in six months, and the contractor who hosted the legacy software application was eager to shut down that system and move on to other ventures. Unfortunately, the project to replace the old software application was failing miserably.

A project management quality assurance (QA) consultant was called to the office of the state agency's IT director and asked if anything could be done to save the failing project. As a result of a series of communications and technical misadventures on the parts of both the agency and the legacy system's host, continuing the relationship with the old vendor beyond the remaining six months was not an option.

The agency was in dire straits. The system replacement project needed to be fixed, pronto, or the agency stood to lose a large piece of its annual budget and face the wrath of constituents who would not be able to get their hunting and fishing licenses on time.

The project manager for the "stuck" effort reported directly to the IT director. The IT director believed that the reporting arrangement was inappropriate, and that the project manager should be more closely aligned with the business unit that operated the system being replaced. The IT director recommended to management that an external QA consultant be retained to provide an objective review of the situation and make recommendations for remediation.

The QA consultant listened to the IT director's story and concluded that the situation was, in fact, dire. When he asked to see the project's charter, schedule, and other project artifacts, the IT director frowned and said, "I wish I could give them to you. They simply don't exist. There's a requirements list somewhere, but the vendor hasn't acknowledged it and is ready to deliver the new system even though we have not agreed to what the new system will provide. We have no idea if the new system will meet our needs. Everyone is frustrated."

The QA consultant next paid a visit to the project manager. He expressed as much frustration as the IT director, but put a different spin on the situation. The project manager thought the project's goals and objectives were obvious: sell hunting and fishing licenses to the public and capture the revenue from those sales. He believed the vendor responsible for delivering the replacement system should, as presumed experts in the industry, know what the system needs to do to support the agency's needs. The project manager felt a charter simply wasn't needed for the project because the outcome was so obvious.

When the QA analyst posed specific questions about the solution the project might deliver—reporting requirements, accounting, how the new system would improve business for the agency, who was to be involved in defining those solutions—the project manager expressed a heightened level of frustration.

"The vendor should know those things," he stated. "They signed up as experts in the industry, as well as expert software developers. Even if I did feel it was necessary to provide them with the detailed requirements for the project, I would not be able to do so. I don't know who the stakeholders are who would help me with that. The business manager works with the vendor and handles all that."

"What has the sponsor told you about the project situation?" the consultant asked.

"Sponsor? I don't know who that person is," the project manager replied. "I work for the IT director. I guess you'd say he is my sponsor, if anyone is."

Undaunted, the QA consultant identified several members of the agency's staff who were responsible for the system's operation and visited them at their desks. When he asked them what they thought the new solution should look like, their responses differed markedly from the project manager's description.

"We need a system that not only sells licenses to the public, but that also provides rich reporting of our sales areas so we can improve service to our customers," one replied. Another added that the agency's scientific staff and enforcement arm would benefit from the information the system gathered if it could identify where people were likely to fish and hunt as well as the species in which those purchasing the licenses were interested.

A system user from the agency's finance and accounting office suggested that the greatest requirement for the new system is to record income and expenses in a way that integrates with the agency's finance and accounting processes. "Without that capability," she said, "the system will be practically worthless. We won't know if we are financially afloat or sinking until it is too late."

Armed with the information gleaned from the interviews, the QA analyst stopped by to meet the project sponsor—the person responsible for the agency's licensing business. She had been with the agency for four months but had never met the project manager. She expressed her own goals for the project and system very clearly. "It's simple," she said. "I want the project done on time so we can collect money to keep this agency afloat. When the 12 months are up, our old system will be shut down. We've burned our bridges with the old system's vendor and there's no way they will keep it going beyond that date. This project must come in on time."

The QA consultant leaned back in his chair. "Everyone in your organization shares that goal," he said. "But they all have different views of what's important for the new system to provide. There's no consolidated vision, no consensus on the project's focus or on what the agency needs the system to provide." He went on to describe to the project sponsor the different views related to him by the IT director and the project manager.

The project sponsor sighed. "But I can see it so clearly," she said.

"Maybe that's the problem," the QA consultant replied. "You can see it, but the rest of your team remains unaware of your vision. Without a consolidated, universally accepted vision, they are each naturally migrating toward what seems important to them. It's like holding a compass in your hand while you're standing in the wilderness in the dark. Lacking specific direction or orientation, you have 359 opportunities to get lost."

The project sponsor grew thoughtful. "How do I fix this?" she asked. "We need this project done on time."

"Let's try an exercise," the consultant suggested, powering up his laptop. He reiterated how simple yet important a project vision statement can be. A good vision statement, he explained, answers four questions:

1. What does the final solution look like?
2. Who will be affected by the new solution?
3. How will things be different once the solution has been implemented?
4. What value will the solution provide?

The sponsor responded quickly. "The first answer is obvious," she said. "It's an IT project, producing an information technology system to sell fishing and hunting licenses to the public."

"Is that really all it is?" asked the consultant. The sponsor sat back in her chair, all ears.

"It's a common mistake, particularly with IT and building projects," the consultant continued. "Let me ask you a few questions: Will the sellers of those licenses need to be trained? Will agency staff need to be trained to use the information produced by the system? Will your organization's business processes need to be modified to support the new system, or will the system be designed to support your existing business processes? Is your agency's infrastructure adequate to support the new system?"

"I see what you mean," the sponsor replied. "When you get right down to it, this project addresses all those things. It's clearly more than an IT project."

The consultant nodded. "IT projects generally work out that way. There's no such thing as an IT project; there are only business projects with large IT components. Let's get the answer to the first vision question nailed down."

He followed up with a few questions about the first of the four essential elements of a good project vision statement:

1. *What the solution will look like*: The new system will be an off-the-shelf software package that supports selling fishing and hunting licenses to the public through retail outlets, which will retain a portion of the fees for handling. The solution will record sales and run them through the agency's financial system; it will then provide data from those sales to support the scientific investigation of wildlife and fishery populations and trends. The system will provide management reports and access to data for use in decision-making processes at the agency and business unit levels. The sellers and

agency staff will receive training to ensure that the system integrates effectively with existing business processes. To avoid the need to build a customized system, those processes may require modification to integrate the capabilities of the software package with the agency's business needs.

The sponsor smiled. "That's a much broader picture than I had in mind, but I see how it fits."

They then turned to the second essential element of the vision statement: Who will be affected by the project's solution? The consultant recorded the sponsor's words as she talked and read back the following response:

2. *Who will be affected by the project:* The new system will impact the retail sellers, the agency's business office, finance and accounting office, and staff scientists who use the data for their studies. The sales system will also directly impact the public buying the licenses and the agency's enforcement staff.

The third element of the vision statement identified how things would be different once the agency implemented the solution. The project sponsor jumped right in with her view of her project:

3. *How things will be different once the solution has been implemented:* The new system will be easy for the retail sellers to set up and use, and it will include self-instruction so that agency staff remains focused on their work, freed from the current deluge of questions posed by the media and the public. Web-based, the system will interface wirelessly with the agency's infrastructure, allowing set-up and support functions to be carried out with ease. Relevant data will be available in near real-time and the agency's financial position will be apparent on a daily basis, with timely access to decision-making tools. Public access to eligibility and game records will be provided online, increasing ease of use and reducing calls to the business office staff.

The project sponsor then eagerly offered, "I know the answer to the last question, about the value the solution will provide to the organization." The consultant typed as the sponsor spoke:

4. *The value the solution will provide to the organization*: The new solution will increase revenue flow, enhance access to information, reduce business office calls, and free up staff for other duties. It will create goodwill with retailers and the public, enhancing the agency's reputation.

The consultant printed out two copies of their notes. As they read them together, the sponsor smiled. "I don't think I ever realized the true scope of this project," she said.

The consultant replied, "Imagine the difficulty your team faced in the absence of a clear vision statement. How could your project manager and project team meet your expectations without a clear description of what you expected from the project? If you, as the project sponsor, can visualize the solution clearly, your team will likely find a way to build it. Without understanding your vision, the team will be thrashing around without any true sense of direction."

The consultant slid his copy across the desk. "Now, sign it. Your signature will let everyone in the agency know that you own this vision statement and that that they can count on what it says as they plan and execute the project over the next few months. You have a very short timeframe for delivery of the new system and all that goes with it. Your team needs all the help it can get from you."

The sponsor scribbled her signature at the bottom of the page. "What now?" she asked.

"Take your vision statement to the project manager. I'm thinking he will be pleased to meet you and see this document," the consultant replied.

The project manager received the vision statement with enthusiasm when the sponsor approached his desk with the

QA consultant at her side. "Thanks," he said after scanning the brief document. "It's a relief to get this from you and to meet you. With this document, I can see clearly where we're headed. I may have more questions for you later, but right now, I have a lot better idea about what it is you want from the project. I can work with this."

Six months later, the project was delivered on time and on budget. In truth, developing clear direction for the project, while it resolved considerable conflict, confusion, and frustration, was only one piece of a three-part effort that proved necessary to save the project. Two more major adjustments were made to the project to ensure its rapid and successful recovery, but nothing had more of an impact on the project manager and the project team than having clear direction from the sponsor. Once they had a course of direction, they could envision the endpoint—and the planning could really begin.

**Lesson Learned**

*For the project sponsor:* If you can see it, we can build it. If you can't see it, we're going nowhere.

# MANAGEMENT AND CONTROL 2

## Can You Prove Your Project's Status?

A senior business analyst was called to the office of the deputy director of a large state agency. The deputy director, who was relatively new at his job, oversaw a major management effort: a large, complex project to redesign the organization's internal business processes. As the new guy in the agency, the deputy director lacked a frame of reference regarding project sponsorship. He intended to rectify this situation as he wrestled with the challenging project.

The project manager for the effort had consistently been reporting positive status regarding the project's scope, schedule, and cost. Despite the favorable reports, the project sponsor felt uncomfortable with the information the project manager provided.

The deputy director explained his situation to the business analyst. Familiar with the project, the business analyst had his own doubts about the project's status, but he kept his concerns to himself. He commiserated with the deputy director, noting that without additional detail, he doubted he could provide much help.

The deputy director glanced at his calendar. "The project manager is due here in a few minutes. Perhaps you could listen to her report with me and offer me some advice once you've heard what she has to say. She has a good reputation as a project manager and seems like a good person, but her reports leave me with more questions than answers. I hesitate to challenge the veracity of her reports, even though I doubt them for some reason. They just don't feel right to me."

The business analyst agreed to sit in on what he assumed would be a project status meeting. The project manager presented herself well, with the poise and confidence of a seasoned professional.

"So, how's the project going?" the project sponsor asked.

"We're about halfway through the project," the project manager replied.

When the project sponsor asked for more details, she added, "We have produced a lot of deliverables that appear to be of good quality."

"That's good," the project sponsor replied. "How's the budget for the project holding up?"

"We're using some of the project's contingency budget, but we should be all right."

The business analyst noticed that the project manager had not brought any written reports or data with her to the meeting. While he admired her apparent confidence, he also sensed that something was lacking.

"I appreciate the update," the project sponsor said. "Would you mind stepping outside for a moment and standing by as I verify a few things?"

"Of course," the project manager replied, closing the office door behind her. The project sponsor turned to the business analyst. "See?" he asked. "She makes it sound like everything's okay, but how can I be sure? She has a good reputation, but I have the feeling I'm not getting the full story. It's always generalizations but no hard evidence. If she says she's halfway through the project, does that mean half of the project's deliverables were delivered and are of good quality, or does it just mean the schedule or budget are half consumed? She came so highly recommended that I hesitate to ask her. I'm not a trained project manager by any stretch of the imagination, but it seems like she should be further along in the project before she has to dip into the contingency. Is using some of the contingency budget a bad thing or not? How can I be sure?"

The business analyst took a few seconds to gather his thoughts before replying. "Using the contingency budget often signals something amiss on a project. It can also mean that she identified risks, appropriately budgeted for them, and then used the contingency she'd set aside to manage those risks. If that proves to be the case, she should be applauded for a great effort. In truth, the project may be on great footing, but with what she provided you today, there is no way to tell."

"There's more to a project than perfunctory updates to the project sponsor," the business analyst continued. "Her job is to manage and control the project. In project management terms, that means knowing where you planned to be at any moment in time, being able to determine exactly where you are compared to that plan, and positioning yourself and your team to influence the difference. She may well be right in what she's saying—or she may not have a clue. With the budget you have for this project and the complexity of what your project team is trying to accomplish, you need to feel comfortable that she has a good handle on things."

The project sponsor raised his hands in frustration. "What do I do? How do I get her to demonstrate that she has a handle on the project?"

"Make one simple request," the business analyst suggested. "When she gives you a report, ask her to prove it."

"Prove it?"

The business analyst nodded. "Ask her to prove that the project is about half done, that half of the project's deliverables are complete and in good order, that she's managing the budget wisely, and that the project really is okay. I'll jot down a list of the things you might ask her for when you call her back in."

The project sponsor accepted the short list of questions from the business analyst and invited the project manager back in. "I'm glad you feel that the project is on such good footing, but I'd like you to demonstrate that to me in an objective manner," he said. "I trust your word as a professional, but a lot rides on the outcome of this project and I need hard-and-fast evidence that everything is actually all right."

She looked surprised at his words. "I'm not sure what you mean."

The project sponsor frowned at her reply and continued. "I'm asking you to back up the status report you just gave me with hard evidence."

The project sponsor paused as he glanced at the list of questions the business analyst had provided. "I'd like you to prove that your project is, in fact, halfway through its schedule and that the budget is in good condition. You can do that by providing me a copy of your updated project schedule."

He continued: "I would also like to see the list of the deliverables you planned to provide through the course of the project, aligned with your schedule, as well as a list of those you have successfully delivered. I also need to see a breakout of what you thought it would cost to develop those deliverables and what they actually cost the organization to produce, with a snapshot of how those expenditures align with your project's work plan."

The project manager dropped her eyes. "I don't have any of those items. Things seem to be going well and the project team is busy. None of our stakeholders are complaining about the deliverables produced by the project team, so I assume all is well. The project team members seem busy and focused. I just check with them from time to time to help remove any roadblocks."

The project sponsor's face began to darken, but he maintained his composure. "I appreciate your judgment of the situation,

## Chapter 2 ■ Management and Control: Can You Prove Your Project's Status?

but there is too much money involved in this project and too much at stake for the organization to manage an effort like your project by feel. I need something more objective that will give me confidence in what you and your team are doing to deliver the solution we need."

The project sponsor paused. "You have three days to prove to me that the project is in the shape you believe it is in. On Monday, I expect you to return to my office and prove to me that you have a handle on your project."

Gesturing toward the business analyst, he added, "If you need any help, I am sure he will be pleased to offer you advice."

The project manager raised her eyes to meet the glare of her project sponsor, nodded, and said "Yes, sir" as she turned and left the office.

The business analyst headed back to his office, but before much time had passed, he got a call from the project manager. He listened to her for several minutes as she complained about the project sponsor's unreasonable demands and how little time she had to pull things together for the Monday report. He then interrupted her monologue: "You are an experienced project manager. I have no idea why you got yourself into the position that you are in, but you need to sort this situation out. You know how projects are run. You know what it takes to ensure that a project is on course. I suggest that you gather the information, regardless of what it costs you time-wise, and be ready to meet the project sponsor on Monday to prove you are the professional project manager we all think you are."

She asked him for the list of items he had identified for the project sponsor. He read them off:

- The project deliverables, with the dates they were provided or will be provided
- Evidence that the deliverables produced by the project were inspected and accepted by a qualified stakeholder

- A timeline identifying when the work was done to produce the deliverables already provided and when the work will be done for those to be provided in the future

- The names of the individuals who will do each piece of work, along with their salary rates and the cost of any materials or equipment they might use, applied to the project's timeline and aligned with each deliverable

- A month-by-month report of how much had been expended on the project for work performed to date, compared against the projected costs for producing the deliverables.

"That's a lot of work," she noted.

"Your project sponsor has asked you to prove that your assessment of the project is accurate. I don't see any way for you to do that other than by producing those basic project artifacts," the business analyst replied. "It's what any reasonable project manager would do throughout the life of a project."

Three days later, the project manager and the project sponsor met again in the sponsor's office. The business analyst joined the meeting at the sponsor's invitation. He wondered how well the project manager had done with the herculean effort of rebuilding a project schedule and budget from scratch, midway through a project, and comparing them to actual performance. He wondered whether she had even attempted to do so.

The project manager handed the project sponsor and the business analyst each a two-page report highlighting what the project team had accomplished, major tasks coming up in the next three months, high-level milestones, budget projections, actual expenditures to date, and an estimate of the schedule and budget requirements for the remainder of the effort.

She then handed each of them a second brief report. That document listed project deliverables, showing which had been completed, when and by whom each had been accepted, and the projected and actual cost for each item.

*Chapter 2* ■ *Management and Control: Can You Prove Your Project's Status?*

Finally, she handed the sponsor and business analyst a thin folder. Inside it was a copy of the detailed project schedule. The schedule appeared "fully loaded" in that it contained detailed task listings for each item to be produced, noted when each was projected for delivery, and identified the project team members responsible for its production. The schedule incorporated each team member's salary rate and itemized lists of planned and actual expenditures for labor and materials that had been completed or were anticipated.

The business analyst scanned each of the documents. From what he saw in those reports and plans, it appeared that exactly half of the deliverables had been provided, with only a slight variance in cost from projections. He took note that a small part of the project's contingency budget had been consumed some months earlier to address a risk.

After allowing the project sponsor and the business analyst time to consider this information, the project manager handed them each a single sheet of paper that summarized the project's status to date:

- An inventory of the project's deliverables showed that 52 out of 100 deliverables had been produced, inspected, and accepted.

- A financial report indicated $1.3 million in actual expenditures against the projected budget of $2.5 million. This projection varied from the budget allocated for the project by less than 10 percent, which was more than covered by the small portion of the contingency budget that the project team had used.

- Eleven months had elapsed on the schedule out of a 24-month schedule. The 52 deliverables provided by the project aligned in nearly exact order with the schedule.

The project sponsor reviewed the file in silence for a few minutes before glancing up to meet the project manager's tired eyes. "You've put in some long days to generate all this information," he said.

She took a deep breath and nodded. "Yes, sir, I have. But I quickly realized that your concern was warranted. The good news is that we are, indeed, halfway through the project, we have spent a small portion of the project's contingency, and we appear to be in good shape."

"I'm glad to hear that," the sponsor replied. "That gives me a lot more confidence in where you and your team are on this complex, risky endeavor. Thank you for your time."

"No, sir," she said. "Thank you for letting me prove myself. If it hadn't been for my project team, things would not have turned out so well. They helped me pull all this together and kept things going while I had my eye off the ball and on my own personal matters. I know better than that, and I won't let you down from here on out. I'll take it as a personal challenge to be able to respond quickly and objectively whenever I give you a project status report and you ask me to 'prove it.'"

The project sponsor and the project manager stood and shook hands before she left the office.

The sponsor turned to the business analyst and said, "You have been a great help. I finally feel like I have a handle on this project, and that my project manager has got things under control. I bet you don't see this sort of situation every day."

The business analyst smiled and chuckled softly. "If only that were true."

> **Lessons Learned**
>
> *For the project manager:* When reporting your project's status, keep it objective.
>
> *For the project sponsor:* When your project manager offers a project status report, make sure he or she can "prove" it.

# Project Team Management

## 3

## Roles and Responsibilities Are Critical

The chief information officer (CIO) for a large corporation called a project management consultant into her office to discuss an important system development project she felt was in jeopardy. The CIO described the project to the consultant—a seasoned young woman with more than $100 million in projects under her belt—to see what might be done to salvage the effort.

The CIO described the project as follows:

- The budget exceeded $15 million for the entire system development project, from initiation to completion.

- The vendor selected to deliver the new system proposed an application service provider agreement and implementation, meaning that the vendor would construct the system, own it, host it, and maintain it. In return, the vendor would receive a percentage of the revenues generated and managed by the new system.

- The vendor had submitted a "perfect" proposal in response to the company's request for proposals sent out to the general market for these types of systems.

- The contract with the vendor did not include either penalties for poor delivery or incentives for optimum performance.

- Communications with the vendor were problematic. When the project manager tried to talk with the vendor's president, he was ignored.
- The project was halfway through a 12-month schedule, although no vendor status report had crossed the CIO's desk in the past six months.
- The vendor had never formally accepted or acknowledged the requirements for the new system.
- The vendor was ready to deliver the new system.
- The organization's business manager was responsible for managing the vendor contract. His staff would depend on the system to generate $75 million in annual revenue, which represented half of the corporation's annual revenue. Together, the vendor and the business manager instituted four changes to the project scope, without a single project modification.
- It was rumored that the business manager and the vendor had agreed to a schedule that no one had seen, which required delivery of the new system in the next two weeks.
- The project manager was a dedicated individual who spent long hours answering emails, filing reports, and writing requirements for the project.
- The project manager reported directly to the CIO.
- The business manager and the project manager had adjacent offices, but never talked.
- The CIO believed she was not the project sponsor for the project and did not know who was.
- The project manager was not sure who was the project sponsor.

The consultant took careful notes during the CIO's briefing. When the CIO finished, the consultant reviewed her notes and replied, "You're right. Your project is in trouble. It sounds to me

*Chapter 3* ■ *Project Team Management: Roles and Responsibilities Are Critical*

like the vendor is out of control and there's no one high up in the organization to rein the vendor in."

The CIO nodded. "I'm pretty sure that would not be me and frankly, I don't have the time or knowledge to manage a project like this. We have only six months left before the old vendor pulls the legacy system offline. I'm not sure this situation can be salvaged."

The consultant replied, "Give me a week or so. I see a few areas right off that might make sense to tackle, but I'd like to check some things out personally, if that's all right."

The CIO nodded. "Of course; whatever you need. If this project fails, we are in deep trouble. The business manager has alienated the vendor that provides our legacy system and the vendor plans to shut down the old system in six months, no matter what."

The consultant continued: "I'll need access to the executive suite. The first thing we need to do is find out who the project sponsor really is. I think you're correct that you are not the right person for the job. In the IT project management world, there is no such thing as an IT project; there are only business projects that deliver an IT system as one component of a larger solution. And that means that the project sponsor has to be a business person rather than a technical resource."

The CIO agreed and made a few calls to ensure that the consultant would be well-received when she arrived at the company's executive headquarters.

The next day, the consultant was welcomed into the CEO's office. As she explained the situation with the project, the CEO, who gave the impression of long years of experience in the industry, smiled politely.

"I know of the situation," the CEO offered. "I authorized payment for your consulting contract. To answer your first question: no, I am not the project sponsor. That would be one of the workshop attendees, and I would like to know exactly who that is once you figure it out. I would also like to be apprised of your findings once you get things in hand."

The CEO's assistant showed the consultant to a long row of offices. The title on the first door read "chief financial officer." She knocked on the door and was beckoned inside. "How can I help you?" the CFO asked.

The consultant explained the project situation, outlining the information the CIO had provided. "Are you the project sponsor for this project?"

"No," she replied. "I am definitely interested, though, since the new system will account for half of our firm's revenue and that is where my interest lies. I hope you'll keep me in the loop."

The consultant smiled to herself as she left the CFO's office. The CEO and CFO were certainly not the right people to sponsor the project, but they were quite interested in its outcome. That spoke well for senior management support. She knew that the keys to any project's success are the leadership team's interest and buy-in.

The consultant worked her way through three more offices, where the director of research and development tacitly denied any interest or involvement, but suggested that the marketing director might be the right person for the job. The marketing director bowed out equally fast, indicating that while he remained interested in the market data the system generated, he was not directly responsible for the project. The chief of production responded similarly. It wasn't until the consultant reached the office of the chief operations officer that she struck pay dirt.

The COO listened to the consultant's story with interest. He frowned when the consultant finished describing the situation and said, "That project is of great interest to me. The business manager works for me. I assumed that the CIO had the situation covered, but I can see that things are pretty much a mess. I am disappointed that the business manager and the vendor seem to be running free and easy with the contract and that we appear to have no control over the requirements. Tell me how you can determine who the right person is for the project sponsor role?"

"The project sponsor is the person in the organization who can write checks and make decisions that stick," the consultant replied. "If something needs to be added to the project's scope, the sponsor approves it or not, and must be willing to write the check, figuratively or literally, to make it happen."

"That would be me, then," the COO responded. I sign those checks for the CFO and pay them monthly out of my budget."

He pulled out a sheet of paper. "It seems to me that the first thing we need to do is figure out what exactly a project sponsor does for a project. After that, I need to talk to the project manager and the business manager and get the vendor in line. Can you help me figure this situation out?"

The consultant scooted her chair up to the COO's desk and pulled out her laptop. She printed out a list of usual roles and responsibilities for a project sponsor, which included the following:

- Act as final authority on escalated issues
- Act as final authority on decisions related to the project budget
- Assume role of business owner responsible for organizational, political, and financial support of the project
- Define strategic vision, assist in project scope management, and convey project importance to internal and external groups
- Run project steering committee meetings
- Define vision, goals, and objectives for the project
- Resolve issues that cannot be resolved at a lower level
- Ensure that the project supports the organization's strategic business direction

- Provide budget accountability and contract signature authority
- Review and approve key project deliverables
- Drive policy decisions for the project
- Communicate with stakeholders, external entities, and partners
- Authorize supplemental personnel resources as required
- Oversee and assist in resolving issues associated with quality, scope, risk, schedule, and budget
- Provide leadership as the project champion
- Approve scope, schedule, and budget changes.

"That is the condensed version," the consultant said. "Perhaps you can keep it as a quick reference."

"That's a help," the sponsor replied. "Do you have something that can help me figure out what the project manager is supposed to be doing?"

The consultant handed the sponsor another list, this one identifying the usual roles and responsibilities of a project manager:

- Report to and take direction from the project sponsor
- Manage and communicate with the vendor to ensure a single voice and focus for the project
- Attend project meetings with the vendor team
- Escalate issues to the project sponsor that cannot be solved at a lower level and may impact the project's schedule, cost, or quality
- Manage the day-to-day tasks performed by the project team

- Manage the deliverable review process to ensure that the delivered solution meets the organization's goals and objectives
- Identify risks and implement risk mitigation strategies
- Facilitate and promote stakeholder communication
- Serve as the point of contact with stakeholder groups
- Monitor the deliverable and milestone schedule
- Maintain project work plans, action item lists, and issue and risk logs for the project team
- Monitor and report overall project status, including the status of all vendor deliverables
- Keep the project sponsor and stakeholders informed of project progress
- Develop and manage statement of work documents
- Determine project resource requirements and enlist stakeholder support to obtain those resources
- Monitor and track project budget, schedule, and quality against defined project objectives
- Oversee ongoing financial administration of the project
- Ensure vendor contract compliance.

Looking through the list, the COO said, "If I'm going to be the sponsor of a project like this one, I'll need one of these people on my team."

"Yes, you will," the consultant replied. "The first thing I'd suggest is that you bring the project manager under your direct control. He works for the CIO right now, and the CIO realizes that the project manager should not be reporting to her for this project. I believe the project manager will benefit from the move as well. Having direct access to the project sponsor opens many doors for timely decision-making, discussion of ideas and issues, and so on. In fact, moving the project manager under your direct supervision is the first step in a chain of activities that may help your project succeed. Let me list a few of those things for you." She offered the following suggestions:

1. *Move management of the vendor under the project manager.* The project manager should have overall responsibility for the project, and that includes everything the vendor does or does not do. Empower the project manager by moving him under your direct control, so that everyone in the organization, including the business manager, realizes that you are serious about your direction.

2. *Assign the project team to work directly for the project manager.* The project manager should be the one voice that gives direction, solves problems the team members cannot work through themselves, and relates your vision and the value of doing this project to the team members.

3. *Modify the contract to include some items that will ultimately enhance the vendor's ability to deliver what you need,* in the timeframe you need it, including the following:

    a. A list of detailed requirements specifying exactly what you expect the new system to provide; include that list in an amendment the vendor must acknowledge contractually. This creates clear expectations and provides a solid baseline for everyone—the vendor and your own team members—to work from.

    b. A schedule that ties every piece of functionality and the delivery of the final system to a specific set of milestones. The details of any schedule will shift a bit, no matter how well you think you have them nailed down, but establish a solid framework for development, testing, and acceptance.

    c. Incentives for exceptional vendor performance and penalties for poor vendor performance. Share the wealth if the vendor gets things done ahead of have no choice but to honor your business manager's direction to us."

"But there's nothing in writing," the project manager protested.

"Doesn't matter," the company president replied. "We are ready to deliver your system. You can take it or leave it."

He gestured toward the door. "This meeting is over."

The consultant got behind the wheel of their rental car and called the COO, who listened quietly and then said, "Head back to your hotel. I'm going to make a few calls."

"Should we move our flights to this evening instead of tomorrow evening?" the project manager asked.

"No. You two get a good night's sleep," the sponsor replied. "Plan to head back to the vendor's offices first thing in the morning."

The next morning, the project manager and consultant were at breakfast when the sponsor called.

"I called the CEO of the holding company that owns the software development firm you visited yesterday and explained the situation," he said. "She turned out to be a very smart, savvy person. The fact that I would rather terminate the contract for the project and suffer the loss—and tell all of my peers in the industry about my experience—than continue with that company seemed to strike a chord with her."

He continued, "The CEO called me back an hour later and explained that she talked to the software company's president and got the same disrespectful attitude you got. She fired him and promoted the vice president. The CEO said she would talk to the new president of the company this morning and have her ready to meet you for lunch at noon. Be there, and then report back to me after your meeting."

At noon, the consultant and the project manager arrived at the software development company. The new president met them at the door and welcomed them into the work bay, where 15 cubicles were now occupied by people who appeared to be very busy.

"We called a technical temp agency and paid top dollar for these resources," she explained. "This morning, I hired a project manager who will be arriving at your site on Monday to work onsite and facilitate the project from your end."

The consultant smiled. "Fast work," he said.

She nodded. "We will do what it takes to honor our contract and deliver your system. Now, if you both have a moment, I would like to sit down and hammer out a contract amendment that meets your needs and addresses your concerns."

Six months later, the project closed with a functional system that met most of the organization's objectives. To recover the project and complete it in such short order, the organization deferred a number of low-priority project objectives and system requirements, and the vendor agreed to an expedited, two-shift, 16-hour development day focused on the customizations and configurations of the software package needed to meet the organization's needs. Plans put into place at the end of the contract cemented both organizations' intent to implement the remaining requirements under a risk-sharing agreement.

When the project drew to a close six months after that first meeting between the project sponsor and the consultant, they were pleased, if a bit frustrated by the level of effort it took to accomplish all that was needed within the six-month timeline.

At project close, the consultant was called in to facilitate a lessons-learned workshop. At the top of the list of lessons learned were the basic project management tenets the project sponsor had implemented at the consultant's suggestion: (1) a direct reporting chain between the project sponsor and the project manager, (2) direct control over the vendor and the project team by the project manager, and (3) specific contractual wording that provided clear guidance and opportunities for all parties to succeed.

> **Lesson Learned**
>
> *For the project sponsor:* Clearly define roles and responsibilities to align a project for success in terms of project management empowerment, reporting authority, and procurement and vendor management.

# Stakeholder Management

# 4

## Consensus Is the Path to Success

A large state agency hired a project quality assurance (QA) analyst for a project that would revolutionize how the state's leadership viewed and used student achievement data to improve high school graduation rates. The project's goal was to increase student achievement through access to student data in the classroom, at the school level, and across the state. The education professionals in the agency, the state legislature, and the governor viewed the project as a priority undertaking that would impact the state's future citizens in a very positive way.

The project sponsor called the QA analyst to join the project because it had stagnated. After more than seven months, the project charter was not yet written or approved and the stakeholders were growing increasingly impatient. The sponsor hoped the QA analyst could suggest ways for the project to regain some badly needed momentum. The state's K–12 education leadership team viewed the situation with a jaundiced eye and demanded corrective action.

The QA analyst met the project sponsor at his office. The sponsor described the situation briefly. "It is my experience that initiating a project, including publishing and approving the project charter, should not take a long time. We are seven months into our three-year schedule for this project and the charter is nowhere in sight."

"Have you identified a reason?" the QA analyst asked.

"I was hoping you might help with that," the sponsor replied.

"I'll need a bit more information before I can formulate any sort of approach for helping the project along," the QA analyst replied.

The sponsor stood. "I could describe the situation in more detail, but it might be better just to show you. The project steering committee is meeting in five minutes. I'd like you to sit in and observe. Afterwards, we can discuss what you saw and any thoughts you might have."

The sponsor and the QA analyst walked to a large conference room, where the tension and anger were palpable. The analyst watched the 11 committee members, all of whom she knew, argue vociferously across the table. All but one of the committee members (the IT manager) possessed a doctorate in their discipline and all were highly paid professionals in the organization who were well-thought of and generally had agreeable personalities.

The project manager arrived late to the meeting and took a seat at the head of the table. He called the meeting to order and handed out the agenda.

"The purpose of today's meeting is to reach consensus about the focus of this project. We need to agree on what the project is to accomplish so that we can get the charter drafted and the project moving."

One of the steering committee members quickly rose from his chair, waving the agenda. "I don't see my topics on this list. Where are the items I provided you when we talked last week?"

Another person interrupted. "I told the project manager to omit the things you gave him. They were senseless, a waste of money and time, and contributed nothing."

The room exploded as members of the committee started shouting at each other. From the QA analyst's perspective, there seemed to be no sense of direction or focus to their concerns or exclamations. The committee ignored attempts by the project manager to return order to the group.

The project sponsor finally interceded. The room quieted as he rose from his chair and walked to the front of the room. "It is obvious that we have made no progress in resolving our differences. I asked the project manager to poll you to identify your expectations. I gather that was either not done or that the effort resulted in even greater confrontation and discord."

The project sponsor glanced at the project manager, who responded with eyes downcast. "I didn't call all of them," he admitted.

"That is unfortunate," the sponsor concluded. "This meeting is adjourned until we can get something done to bring you all together on this project, or we shut it down and return the federal funding we worked so hard to get to make this project a reality."

One of the more senior of the steering committee members squared off with the project sponsor from across the table: "You can't shut this thing down. It means too much."

The sponsor, with a carefully neutral expression, replied, "I will not see this project fail because of your inability to come together as a governing body. If it is the right thing to do, I will indeed shut this project down."

The committee members filed out the door grumbling, "We'll never get this project done...." "Incompetent project manager...." "Projects always fail around this place...."

After everyone had left, the project sponsor took a seat at the conference table and faced the QA analyst. "Do you see the problem here?"

The QA analyst nodded. "Your stakeholders are running amok, and I'm surprised to see that. I know most of them from past projects and they are good people—highly skilled, motivated professionals. What's going on?"

"The project manager cannot seem to bring them together, and I'm not doing any better. You saw the results. We've been doing this for months without a single step forward. I know that you not only do QA, but that you are a skilled project manager and facilitator. I'd like you to help if you can."

The QA analyst shook her head. "As an external QA professional, I'm paid to stand outside the project and make recommendations. I don't generally get involved directly. I can make some suggestions…."

The project sponsor interrupted her. "I appreciate your position, but this is an exceptional situation. I need your help. This is an important project that will impact students directly. We need this project to succeed."

The QA analyst nodded. "There is something I may be able to do without getting too directly involved that might help move the project forward."

She went on to describe the process she would use to try to get things on course. The project sponsor was pleased. "Your plan sounds like a good one. Without a doubt, it can't hurt to try. Can you begin immediately?"

The next day, the QA analyst met again with the project sponsor. Together, they crafted a clear vision statement that identified:

- What the solution looked like from the project sponsor's perspective
- How things would be different once the solution was implemented
- Who would be impacted by the project
- The value the project sponsor and the organization expected to realize from the project.

The sponsor gladly signed the document, which the QA analyst scanned and emailed to each member of the project's steering committee along with a copy of the project sponsor's vision statement. The analyst requested a meeting with each stakeholder during the coming week.

The response from the steering committee members was positive. They each welcomed the visit from the QA analyst, indicating their interest in seeing the project succeed and determination to move beyond the current conflict to more productive ground.

For the next week, the QA analyst made appointments and interviewed each of the 11 steering committee members at their offices. The meetings, which lasted no more than 45 minutes, focused on each stakeholder's perceptions of the project sponsor's vision statement as well as the specific business value and capabilities each believed the project should deliver.

When the QA analyst met the first steering committee member, a woman near the end of a 40-year career in education, she could feel the intensity of her concern for the project's success and her anxiety over its current lack of momentum. The committee member had doctorates in curriculum development and early education and was recognized nationally as an expert in her field.

The QA analyst opened the interview by expressing her thanks for the committee member's time and then launched into the purpose of the meeting. "What I'd like to do first is get your take on the project sponsor's vision of what this project is supposed to deliver."

The committee member was eager to respond, but the QA analyst elaborated before hearing her out. "What I would really like is to identify your vision for this project in terms of what the solution might look like, who will be affected by it, how things will be different once it is implemented, and the value it will provide to this agency and the state. It's okay to disagree with the project sponsor, but we need to ensure that we are all working off the same sheet of music. I can assure you that the project sponsor welcomes your feedback."

The committee member paused, scribbled a few notes on a piece of paper, and then slid it across the table. On that piece of paper were explicit answers to each of the four questions the QA analyst had posed. The QA analyst reviewed the notes. "It seems like you've given this a lot of thought, and that your vision of the project's outcome mirrors the sponsor's vision."

"You bet," the committee member replied. "I find it hard to believe that the steering committee members and I actually disagree on what's needed for this project. But I have to admit that I have never had the question of a project vision statement put to me quite like you did. Your questions helped me focus my thoughts."

"Thanks," the QA analyst replied. "But I'd like to ask you to address one more aspect of how you see things turning out for the project."

The committee member leaned forward in her chair. "Shoot," she said.

"I'd like you to help me define the objectives for the project," the QA analyst started.

She raised a hand to hold off what appeared to be a ready answer from the committee member. "In project management, objectives may be a bit different from what you have encountered in the past, with strategic objectives and such. Objectives—in the project management lexicon—are statements of the value the project will provide. By definition, once a project's objectives are achieved, the project is done. Everything that is built or developed for the project, from software to reports to employee training, ties directly to an objective or it will be considered out of scope. So the things I'm asking you to define are all important."

The committee member's expression shifted from enthusiasm to quiet consideration and thought.

The QA analyst continued. "Project objectives are specific and focus on a single, narrowly defined aspect of the solution to be provided by the project. They are measurable in that they can be quantified and they provide a tangible benefit that can be objectively identified once an objective has been met. They are assignable to one or more specific stakeholders—someone like you, who signs up to sponsor that objective and own the details of the requirements the project team builds to satisfy the objective. As the owner of an objective, you guide the development and delivery of that objective. Objectives are realistic in that they are time-bound, meaning that they are delivered during the course of the project."

The committee member nodded her understanding. "I like the concept. Can you give me an example?"

"Sure," the QA analyst responded. "Consider this as a possibility, particularly given the project sponsor's vision statement: 'Provide a tool that will gather and report data on student achievement for all 9th-grade students attending public schools, immediately prior to matriculation to the high school level, for science, math, and reading comprehension. This tool will be accepted by the sponsoring stakeholder as a part of final user acceptance of the new system.'"

The QA analyst paused, and then added, "Now let's take that objective apart and see if we have the components needed for it to qualify as a good project objective."

She scribbled the letters S, M, A, R, and T vertically down the left side of a piece of paper and then filled in the pieces of the objective that aligned with each element:

- **S (specific):** a tool that will gather and report data on student achievement for all 9th-grade students attending public schools, immediately prior to matriculation to the high school level, for science, math, and reading comprehension.

- **M (measurable):** for all 9th-grade students attending public schools. The emphasis is on "all," which is quantifiable for any school district and the state.

- **A (assignable):** assigned to the stakeholder being interviewed.

- **R** (realistic): seems like this is well within technological capabilities, given that school districts and the state already gather enrollment data for students in all grades who attend public school.
- **T** (time-bound): to be accepted by the sponsoring stakeholder as a part of final user acceptance of the new system.

The stakeholder then drew her own matrix on another piece of paper. "I like the concept," she said.

She drew several rows across down the width of the paper, and listed the SMART letters down the left side.

"First, let me sign up for the objective you just provided; it's right on the money. Second, let me fill in another objective or two using your SMART model."

The stakeholder began scribbling notes on each row that aligned with each letter of SMART. When she was done, she slid the paper across the table to the QA analyst.

The QA analyst read the notes, asked a few clarifying questions, and realized that her first interview had provided four very clear, articulate objectives that were specific, measurable, assignable, realistic, and time-bound.

She glanced up at the committee member with increased respect. "Those are great. This has got to be the easiest interview I have ever held. You've given me exactly what I was looking for."

The committee member responded, "No, it's me who should be thankful. You made it easy. How you structured your vision statement question and then laid out a format for the project objectives described a model I could relate to easily. In the field of education, we deal with teaching models every day. It's our bread and butter. Your questions talked right to my sweet spot."

The QA analyst thanked the committee member for her time and hurried off to her next interview. Before arriving at the next

*Chapter 4 ■ Stakeholder Management: Consensus Is the Path to Success*

person's office, she took a few minutes to print out a copy of the vision statement and the objectives developed during the first interview. When she arrived at the next committee member's office, she began her discussion much the same way as the first, but asked this person to take a look at the vision statement and modify it to suit her perspective of the project. With a few word changes, the interviewee accepted the vision statement as written.

When the conversation turned to project objectives, the QA analyst used the objectives from the first interview as a starting point. The interviewee received all four objectives as complete and accurate, and added several more to the list. As the interview drew to a close, the committee member made some positive remarks and expressed gratitude to the QA analyst for helping her crystallize her vision of what the project was to provide as well as her activity's specific needs.

This process continued with each of the steering committee members through the rest of the week. With the exception of the IT manager, the committee agreed on the vision statement with few modifications. Through the interviews, 14 project objectives were identified, four of which appeared to be core concerns for the committee membership as a whole.

When the QA analyst showed the project sponsor the vision statement and list of objectives at the end of the week, he was very excited. "Who would have guessed?" he said as he looked over the list. "After all that arguing, for seven frustrating months, you came up with this over the course of five days."

"A lot of that had to do with the steering committee members making themselves available to me on such short notice," the QA analyst replied. "Their responsiveness suggests that while they may not have gotten along on this project in the past, they all perceive it as important enough to make time in their schedules to address the project's needs."

The sponsor set the vision and objectives document aside and leaned back in his chair. "I can see how you might reach that conclusion, but we have a way to go before we can charter this project and get moving."

The QA analyst shook her head. "On the contrary, I believe you are very close to doing exactly that. Here's my plan for bringing this issue to a head and getting some traction on the project."

A week later, the QA analyst and the project sponsor called the steering committee members together for a two-hour project vision and objectives workshop. They split into two groups of six, with the project sponsor serving as the sixth member on one of the groups. Each workgroup was given a copy of the vision statement and asked to discuss it and validate it as the governing vision statement for the project. In anticipation of the workshop, the QA analyst had modified some wording and eliminated a few elements of the solution's description.

At the end of the first hour, the committee members reconvened and presented their updated versions of the vision statement to the QA analyst. More than one knowing glance was cast toward the analyst, whom all concluded had inadvertently changed the vision statement from what they had seen during the individual interviews and in the material sent out in advance of the workshop. The QA analyst acknowledged that she had revised the wording and made the suggested changes. She loaded the corrected vision statement into her laptop and projected it on the screen at the front of the room.

After giving everyone a few minutes to review the vision statement, she called for a vote to determine the group's acceptance level. The vote was unanimously in favor.

For the second hour of the workshop, the steering committee workgroups reviewed the list of project objectives the QA analyst had developed through her interviews. Again, the wording of the objectives had been modified to get the attendees' attention and determine their level of commitment to the exercise. When the workgroups gathered together at the end of the hour, the QA analyst took numerous good-natured jabs regarding her "carelessness" in recording and reporting the objectives.

Once again, the QA analyst projected the results of the steering committee's efforts on the screen and gave the attendees a few minutes to review the final wording. Again, vote was unanimously in favor.

The committee member the QA analyst had interviewed first spoke up and said, "I believe this list warrants one more correction before we call this workshop to a close. I think we need to include a statement indicating that this vision statement and list of objectives will guide the project's scope from here forward, and they cannot be changed without the project sponsor's approval, which will be given after consultation with this committee."

Everyone nodded in agreement.

Two weeks later, the project charter was completed. The budget, schedule, roles and responsibilities, risks, and other elements of the document proved relatively easy to develop once the committee had reached consensus on the main issues.

Two weeks after that, the project sponsor, a new project manager (the first one was let go), and each member of the steering committee signed the project charter. From that point on, even though discussions were sometimes intense and animated, the steering committee functioned as a group with one direction and purpose.

Two and a half years later, the project was delivered on schedule with all objectives met and signed off on by each of the steering committee members.

> **Lesson Learned**
>
> *For the project manager:* Consensus breeds success and a smooth project. Use the steering committee members' experience and expectations to guide the project to ensure progress and likely success.

# PROJECT INITIATION

## 5

# Get Your Project Off to a Good Start

Debbie Spaulding, PMP

A large state agency was awarded funding for a multimillion-dollar project to modernize and focus business processes that were mired in old-school methodology and outdated legacy systems. Years of struggle at this agency to build software that would streamline business processes and automate much of its work had resulted in cobbled-together systems that fell short of meeting business needs.

The agency had a well thought-out general IT strategic plan to resolve this situation, which had executive-level support, but struggled to navigate its culture of siloed operations and shortsighted software and IT priorities. To add to the complexity of the situation, the agency was heavily dependent on federal funding, and political party leadership changes that drove funding and reprioritizations often resulted in unpopular initiatives with no funding, inconsistent backing, and virtually no chance of implementation.

In 2006, the agency won a significant grant to make sweeping changes to many of its core systems at the enterprise level. The problem was that only a few programs in the agency were thinking "enterprise." Other areas, especially those that were starving for funds, continued to politick and posture for their projects. Some rallied for systems that were clearly out of the scope of the grant, demanding their piece of the project pie.

Something had to be done or the grant money would be lost and the agency would miss an important opportunity to move forward in support of its key mission and goals. The CIO and the manager of the project management office came together and developed a strategy for addressing the situation before it was too late. Their intent, they agreed, was to bring consensus to the project so that it might be initiated effectively, increasing its chances for success.

An eight-hour off-site workshop was organized. Representatives of all departments were required to attend and an independent consultant was brought in to facilitate. The goals of the workshop were to define the following related to the grant the agency had received:

- The enterprise-level values that would drive the project's goals and objectives
- The specific stakeholders who would be engaged directly as part of the project approach
- The vision the project would fulfill
- The specific scope of the project.

The facilitator started by tactically unifying the workshop attendees. They discussed their common concerns, including duplicative requests for project funding and the redundancy of work processes between their departments. The facilitator then moved the attendees into a review of the conditions of the grant that would fund the project, so that they could decide on exactly what the money would be used for. Once the discussion started, consensus was quickly achieved on both points. Arguments and complaints dissipated as the group came together on key aspects of what the project would strive for and how that might be achieved.

The task of determining exactly which stakeholders would be involved in the project proved to be long and complex.

Ultimately, more than 100 stakeholders were identified and the challenges of managing such a large, diverse group were discussed. To minimize conflict within the stakeholder group of interested professionals, attendees at the workshop determined that stakeholders would be engaged in the following manner:

- Stakeholder ownership for projects would be methodically determined to ensure clear responsibility for the business area addressed by the project. Stakeholder identification would focus on:
    o What is their interest and why?
    o What is at stake for them?
    o What is their influence while the project is underway?
    o What is their influence on the product or service once the project is completed?
    o What is their influence on future projects or products?
- Stakeholders would be held responsible for the ultimate success or failure of the project, given the specific need for their engagement, decisions, and feedback to the project team.

The workshop attendees agreed that the stakeholders define project success. The challenge was how to manage them, recognizing that stakeholders usually have competing visions, needs, and priorities.

After the workshop attendees identified the project stakeholders, they focused on their departmental agendas. In group exercises, they presented their agendas and tied them back to the enterprise plan. Through this open communication, the group realized that by working together they could redefine and prioritize elements of the project scope to create an enterprise vision. With the grant parameters in front of them and a greater understanding of the agency's enterprise vision, attendees were able to define which parts of the larger vision should be the focus of the grant opportunity—and which parts should not be included.

The attendees, as the organization's leaders, were then able to articulate scope and vision and, more importantly, sell the scope and vision to their respective stakeholders with enthusiasm and confidence. With the vision and scope firmly in hand, the workshop attendees declared victory and expected to call it a day—but they weren't done yet.

The final task for the workshop was to create a communication plan that would relate the vision and scope of the project to the organization. The vision and scope were clearly identified and the list of stakeholders had been defined, so that task was easily completed. Attendees identified which stakeholders would be most closely involved in the project and which would not be directly involved in the effort. This understanding would enable them to define, focus, and disseminate project-related communications.

By sequestering the directors of this large agency, focusing their efforts to define a project to meet key organizational goals, and facilitating their efforts along focused lines, intra-agency bickering gave way to collaborative efforts, setting the project up for success. Had the organization failed to take this step, consensus and collaboration would not have been achieved, making the project's success much less likely.

> **Lesson Learned**
>
> *For the project sponsor:* During the initiation of any project where stakeholder goals and objectives are wide and diverse—and politically influenced—extraordinary means must be taken. Without extraordinary effort to overcome these obstacles, the project's chances for a good beginning and, ultimately, for success, are greatly diminished.

# COMMUNICATIONS MANAGEMENT

# 6

## Don't Let Tech-Speak Threaten Your Project

A large private sector company hired a seasoned project management consultant to mentor its staff through a complex web redesign project. The deputy CEO appointed himself both the project sponsor and the project manager for the effort. Although he realized he had limited time to devote to the project, he felt the project's importance demanded his personal attention. He designated his executive assistant to act as his deputy project manager, primarily to handle the paperwork and scheduling. The CEO had little project management experience, so he counted on the consultant to ensure that he and his team moved their project deliberately and successfully from initiation to completion.

The project scope included rebuilding the company's internal website for staff and external website for customers and stakeholders. The project was complex, with components that included information technology, business analysis, customer relationship management, document management, marketing, and electronic commerce.

For the first six months, the project moved ahead satisfactorily. The schedule proved realistic and achievable, and stakeholders generally provided timely input for the website design and development team to accomplish their tasks on schedule and with good results. Unfortunately, at the halfway point, the CEO was recruited by another company to take over as its company president, a position he accepted immediately. With his departure, the project no longer had a sponsor or a project manager.

The executive assistant showed up at the consultant's office on a gray Monday morning to inform the consultant of the CEO's sudden departure. In the absence of other options, the company's management group had designated her as the replacement project manager and the president of the company as the project's sponsor. Given the president's other pressing duties, sponsor engagement was likely to be lower than it had been to date. The panic in the executive assistant's voice was evident as she asked the consultant "What am I going to do? I'm not a project manager, let alone an IT expert. I'm an administrative assistant."

The consultant tried to reassure her. "First," he started, "you know the business of the company. You have been the CEO's executive assistant for many years. If anyone has a good grasp of the workings of the company and the people who are involved, it is you. Second, this is not an IT project. It is a business project with a large IT component, intended to satisfy a business need."

The consultant paused as the assistant considered his words, and then continued. "As an executive assistant, you have managed projects for your entire career. It is what executive assistants do. Think of all the assignments you have tackled. Each one of them was a project. Further, you have watched us set up and organize this project, and you have intimate knowledge of the project's schedule. I'm here to help you whenever you need it, but you definitely have what it takes to launch the new websites six months from now."

The executive assistant shook her head in frustration. "But they use so many technical terms. It's all tech-speak to me. If I can't understand what they're saying, how can I possibly manage the project?"

The consultant considered his words carefully before continuing. "Don't doubt that this is an opportunity. Very few people are qualified to meet the need for experienced, trained project managers. This is a great opportunity for you to gain experience

*Chapter 6  ■  Communications Management: Don't Let Tech-Speak Threaten Your Project*

in a highly marketable field and deliver real value to your organization."

Her expression suggested that she was dubious regarding the opportunity, but the consultant assured her. "Effective communication underpins the success or failure of every project. Your concern about understanding and being able to talk with your technical team is a common issue for projects of all kinds: IT, training, policy, construction, and so on."

"So what do I do?" she persisted.

"Try this," the consultant replied. "Whenever a member of your team uses a term you don't understand, or that anyone at a meeting doesn't understand, make the speaker stop and explain the term in words that are clear to everyone. Then add that term to a list and jot down the definition. Bring the list of terms and definitions to every meeting and pass it around for everyone to use. Continue to update the list whenever team members use new terms and acronyms."

"That's a great idea," the assistant replied. "But won't that slow down meetings?"

"It may slow things down at first, but as everyone learns how to interpret each other's words correctly, you will find that the clarity you achieve as a group will increase, and that your meetings will become more efficient," said the consultant. "What you will also find, based on my experience, is that as the team members realize they must explain themselves every time they use a technical term, they will start speaking in lay terms. All the team members, whether speaking or listening, will become more effective communicators and you will understand what they are saying."

The executive assistant returned to her office to consider the consultant's advice. The next day, she held her first team meeting as the official project sponsor. Five minutes into the meeting, the first technical term came up. As advised, she stopped the conversation and requested an explanation of the term. Several other team members disputed the definition provided, asked clarifying questions, and refined the term's meaning. Once they came to consensus on a modified definition, the executive assistant recorded the term and definition on her list.

This process continued until a half dozen terms had been defined and recorded. The meeting, scheduled for one hour, adjourned slightly later than anticipated.

The consultant overheard one of the business team member's comment as he exited the meeting, "This is the first time I have actually understood what was being said in these meetings and felt like I could make a contribution."

After two months under the new project manager's guidance, the project remained on budget and on schedule for a successful delivery. An important technical review meeting was scheduled to confirm the final plan and architecture for the website, as presented by the vendor contracted to construct both websites for the organization.

As the consultant reviewed a high-level diagram of the website's architecture, he noted arrows indicating that data would flow from several sources into what the vendor identified in an architectural drawing as a "feedlot." Unable to restrain himself, the normally quiet consultant let out a loud laugh. The vendor's project manager raised his eyes in concern. "You find something humorous about the website design?"

"I do," the consultant replied. "What in heaven's name is this feedlot in the website's architecture? I grew up on a farm. We raised sheep, cattle, and pigs for market, and we had a feedlot. It was a muddy, smelly, nasty place that my parents made me work in whenever I misbehaved. I know exactly what a feedlot is. I have never seen the term used in a technical document describing a website."

The vendor glanced at the project manager nervously. "It's one of the novel terms our company uses to bring character to our designs and lighten discussions during the design review process," he replied.

*Chapter 6 ■ Communications Management: Don't Let Tech-Speak Threaten Your Project*

"What is it really?" she asked.

The vendor's project manager looked chagrined as he said, "It's a term we use for data stores."

"Now that's something I understand. And I think it is one of the standard terms identified for use in this project," the consultant replied.

The project manager pointed at the list of terms she had built for the project over the last few months. Each attendee at the meeting had a copy of the list. "Yep, it's in here," she noted.

The consultant continued. "The truth is that you can call your data store Joe, Sam, or Sally, as long as you define your terms. Since this design document is in near-final form, I see little need for you to re-label your feedlots throughout the document, as long as we all understand what the term means."

The project manager chimed in. "I have recorded the term and cross-referenced 'feedlot' with 'data store' in our project's glossary of terms."

Everyone around the conference table shared a laugh, including the vendor.

Four months after the feedlot meeting, the project team implemented the company's new websites. The executive assistant, with the help of the project management consultant, effectively organized the project team, ensured clear communications during project activities, executed a realistic schedule, and implemented the new websites. The two websites received rave reviews from company employees and customers alike.

While ensuring clear communications was not the total answer to the challenges the project faced along the way, it facilitated understanding and ensured clarity of requirements, tasks, objectives, and efforts. Based in part on her success as the project manager, the former executive assistant was hired by

51

her former boss to become a project manager at his new firm. To this day, they both attribute much of the project's success to the simple process of making sure that everyone remained clear about the project's communications.

> **Lesson Learned**
>
> *For the project manager:* Avoid the use of technical terms when at all possible. It is a good bet that many people working in an organization do not understand them. Seek clarity in communications. When you don't understand a term, define it. When you define it, record it. Clear communications foster project success.

# QUALITY MANAGEMENT   7

## Make Quality Your Priority

About to enter his project sponsor's office for the first time, the new project manager reviewed what he knew about the project he had been contracted to manage. The $15 million project had a large IT component and a training piece, and it involved a significant effort to streamline system maintenance and business processes. What he knew about the project could be summarized as follows:

- The project's estimated cost was $15 million to implement.
- The project was halfway through a 12-month schedule.
- The former project manager was very dedicated, spending long hours answering emails, filing reports, and writing requirements, but he was reassigned because of the project's lack of forward momentum.
- The full project team had never met.
- The project did not have a written project charter or project plans such as a communication plan, change management plan, issue management plan, and risk management plan.
- The project sponsor had received numerous calls from constituents throughout the state who were very interested in the project but had heard nothing and were ready to go to their legislators.
- The project did not have a written schedule.

- The vendor had never provided a project status report.
- There was no list of issues or risks that needed to be addressed.
- The requirements for the new system had been written but had never been formally accepted or acknowledged by the vendor.
- The vendor was ready to deliver the new system.

The new project manager knew the project was in trouble and had minimal time available for recovery, and he thought he knew what might get it back on track. But first he needed to find out what the project sponsor expected from the project.

The project sponsor welcomed him into her spacious office. She had earned her senior position through hard work and solid leadership but had been in her new position at the agency for only a month.

"What can I do for you?" she asked as the project manager entered her office. "This is your first day on the job, isn't it?"

The project manager nodded and sat down opposite the project sponsor at a small conference table. "I've had a few days to look over some project artifacts and talk with some of the users of the system that's being replaced," he began. I'm here to get some initial guidance about your expectations for the project."

The sponsor laughed, but there was no humor in her eyes. "What I want is the new system delivered on time and on budget."

"Of course," the project manager replied. "But to my knowledge, the scope of the project has never actually been defined. We could deliver something by using up the rest of the project's budget and schedule, but there is considerable risk that it would not meet your expectations for the system. To complicate things further, the vendor is ready to deliver the system, even though the project requirements have yet to be approved."

The project sponsor, obviously frustrated by where the conversation was headed, responded tersely. "What I want is a quality product from this project. Anything short of good quality is unacceptable."

"That's a start," the project manager replied, careful to keep his tone level and open. "I would like to use this meeting with you to define exactly what quality means in this case."

The project sponsor asked, "Can't you get that information from someone else?"

The project manager shook his head as he started up his laptop. "I really can't get that information from anyone but you. As the project sponsor, you own the scope that defines what will and will not be built on this project. The information you provide will tell me what is in and what is out of consideration for the project team and our vendor to work on, build, and deliver. You are the only one who can commit and approve expenditures for the project. From that standpoint, you are the only one who can make decisions that stick. Without concrete guidance from you about what you want out of the project, we risk others pushing their own agendas, changing the project's direction, and generally creating mayhem."

The project sponsor sighed. "I guess that makes sense. Exactly what do you need from me?"

The project manager handed her several pieces of paper. "Based on what I have gleaned from your stakeholders and system users, I have crafted a draft vision statement and set of objectives. I've also taken the set of requirements the previous project manager developed and aligned them with the project objectives. Each requirement—each thing we build for this project—can now be tied to a specific value statement for the project and linked to one or more stakeholders who own that project objective. What I've found is that at least a third of the requirements for the project do not appear to support this draft vision and list of objectives. I need your review and approval of the vision and objectives so we can get a handle on the project's scope. Once we have that, we can align each requirement with a specific objective and stakeholder. We will identify those that don't align as out of scope."

An hour later, the project manager left the sponsor's office with an approved vision statement and list of objectives for the project. During the course of their meeting, the sponsor had made a few modifications to the vision statement but had generally accepted it as defined by the new project manager. She had also added an objective to the list and eliminated an objective that she considered a political ploy by a stakeholder to end-run his boss.

With those two documents in hand, the project manager went back to his office and got to work. First, he analyzed the project's requirements, working with project team members to link each requirement to a project objective. He then worked with the team to develop a strategy to fulfill the sponsor's vision, achieve the project's objectives, and satisfy the requirements. Once the strategy was developed, he directed the team members to estimate the work and resources needed to achieve the objectives, sequence the work, and develop a new project schedule. Human and material resources were assigned costs and an estimated budget for the project was established.

Over the course of their effort, the project team developed much of what was needed for a brief project charter. The project manager took all the information, along with the new project schedule, and headed to his second meeting with the project sponsor.

As he handed the project sponsor a copy of the new project charter, including the schedule and budget estimate, he explained, "In the project charter you will find the vision statement and objectives approved in our last meeting, along with a list of high-level requirements the project team and I developed based on the list of requirements provided by the former project manager. You can see that the requirements list is now much shorter."

"What happened to the rest of the requirements?" the project sponsor asked.

"They were extraneous, out of scope. That documentation was retained for future use, but at this point, we don't plan to address those deliverables," the project manager replied.

The project manager continued. "The last time I was here, you said you wanted a quality system from this project. By definition, project quality equates to delivering the approved scope for the project within the approved budget and schedule constraints. Based on what's in the project charter, I estimate that we will need an additional four months to deliver that scope but that we can do it within the approved budget. That is all spelled out in the project charter. Once you sign it, approving the project as the team and I have defined it, we can proceed. We feel pretty confident about our chances for success."

"You need four more months?" the sponsor asked.

"We do," the project manager replied, explaining how he and the project team had constructed the detailed schedule.

The project sponsor spent several days reviewing the project charter, budget, and schedule herself and with several key project stakeholders. She then called the project manager to her office to discuss the project charter with him. "This is a very good document," she said. "For as short a time as I have been here, I feel like I at least have a pretty clear vision of what this project entails. I have signed the charter and am authorizing you to take the four additional months you requested. Based on what you've provided me in the charter, I can see that if I want the outcome we need from this project, and if I want the scope satisfied, it will probably take all of that schedule and the budget that we have."

"We call that the triple constraint," the project manager replied. "Scope, schedule, and cost are inherently tied together. If you had told me we could not have the additional four months, I would have asked you which project objectives and requirements you didn't want us to build. We would have still delivered a quality product, but with a scaled-back scope."

"I get it," the sponsor replied. "If you have enough time, as you estimated it, your team can deliver the scope of this new system, including the training and business analysis elements, and that means we get a quality product. If we cut cost or schedule but not scope, or any other combination of the three, we will put the project's quality in jeopardy."

"That's right," the project manager agreed.

"What about how the project is run?" the sponsor asked. "Doesn't that have an impact on quality?"

"It does," replied the project manager. "What we've talked about so far is product quality, but there are more dimensions to quality than that. Without an efficient and effective project management approach, which includes managing our stakeholders, our project team, and our vendor, we will likely fail to deliver the project's scope in the manner we anticipate at this time."

The project manager reached into his briefcase and pulled out another document. "This is a project approach that defines how we will analyze and manage our stakeholders, incorporate the members of the project team into the effort, bring the vendor into line, and manage any changes to our project scope."

"To avoid scope creep, you mean," the sponsor suggested.

"Exactly," the project manager replied. "With those things in place, along with issue management, budget management, and a few other project management tools, we can ensure quality delivery of all the parts of the solution. I would appreciate your taking a look at our project management plan and providing me with your comments. We could meet at another time and walk through the important parts, if you like," the project manager concluded, setting the document on the table.

"I don't have a lot of time in my schedule to review detailed plans," the sponsor said. "Can you set up a briefing for me and some of the key project stakeholders and hit the high points for us?"

*Chapter 7* ■ *Quality Management: Make Quality Your Priority*

"Of course," replied the project manager. "And I appreciate your interest and attention to this project. While it is definitely in trouble at this point, with your support and the project team's efforts, these plans can help us pull it out of the fire and make it successful."

"I believe you may be right," replied the project sponsor. "I feel like we really have a handle on things, given what you've shown me here. I said I wanted quality, and I can see that you are prepared to provide both a quality product and a quality approach to delivering the project's scope. I feel a lot better about the project today than I did two weeks ago. Nice work."

The project manager thanked the project sponsor and headed back to his office. Eight months later, the project was delivered two months ahead of schedule, to positive reviews by stakeholders, system users, and the agency's senior management team. It went into the books as an example of a project that provided a quality solution and real value for the organization.

> **Lessons Learned**
>
> *For the project manager:* Project quality means delivering scope within budget and schedule, with that scope well defined when the project is chartered.
>
> *For the project sponsor:* Demand quality, but understand what that means.

# TIME MANAGEMENT   8

## Schedules Are Guides for Those Who Do the Work

The chief information officer called the external quality assurance analyst into her office at the end of a long, hard day. The project they had just finished had not been an easy one, although it should have been. Scheduled to take six months, the project to conduct a feasibility study took nine months to complete.

The QA analyst wondered about the purpose of the meeting, as the CIO had approved the final report a week earlier. He waited for the CIO to start the conversation.

"I need your feedback on the project we just finished," the CIO said.

The QA analyst shifted uncomfortably in his chair and asked, "Was the final QA report insufficient? I thought it was pretty inclusive. If there are any changes you would like made...."

The CIO waved off the analyst's words. "The report was fine. I need your input on a personnel matter. It's the project manager. I've had some comments from others on the project team as well as from some important stakeholders who interacted with her."

The QA thought back to the project and the many findings and recommendations for improving leadership of the project. He recalled meeting the project manager on the first day of the effort. She had come across as both sincere and professional, leaving the QA analyst hopeful about the outcome of the project. The project manager had said all the right things, particularly about laying out a good project approach and schedule and monitoring progress at an appropriate level.

But that conversation had turned out to be the only interaction he had with the project manager over the course of the project that was civil or professional.

The CIO interrupted the analyst's thoughts and said, "I see you're reflecting. What are you thinking?"

"I've never seen a better project charter or project management plan," responded the analyst. The content in both those documents was appropriate and was adeptly scaled to meet the needs of a small project like a feasibility study. The schedule was detailed to a level I have seldom seen over the last four or five years of providing external quality assurance for projects. It may even have been a better schedule than I ever made for projects I personally managed."

The CIO nodded her head, prompting the analyst to continue.

"Although it seems counterintuitive, that schedule may have been the cause of most of the issues encountered by the project team and may even account for the project's late completion."

"I read that in your report," the CIO replied. "That's why I asked you here. Did the project manager build that schedule in isolation? I mean, did she do it on her own, without any input from the team?"

The QA analyst shook his head. "No. She did that well. She solicited and incorporated everyone's input into the schedule, and planned it to a very detailed level."

The CIO frowned. "That sounds right. So, how could the schedule be the issue, then?"

# Chapter 8 ■ Time Management: Schedules Are Guides for Those Who Do the Work

"You and I both have a lot of projects under our belts, right?" the analyst prompted.

"Too many, I sometimes think," the CIO replied.

"And we both know how projects get done, right?"

"Usually late and over budget," the CIO replied.

The QA analyst smiled. "You're thinking of kitchen remodeling projects," the analyst offered, knowing the CIO was currently in the midst of such an effort.

"Very funny," the CIO replied, nodding for the QA analyst to continue.

"No matter how many tools we use in managing projects, no matter how many plans we write, or how we schedule things, it is people who get projects done," the QA analyst said. "Tools help us organize an effort. But people, by their inherent, complex nature, insert variables into the best of plans—so whatever plans we make must be flexible and adaptable to address those variables. Tasks that a team estimated at one point may change and morph over time as the people on the project team learn more about the effort and the solution they are chartered to deliver. One task grows beyond what was anticipated. Another task reveals itself to be easier to complete than expected."

"That's the normal course of events on projects," the CIO noted. "We call it progressive elaboration."

"Right," the QA analyst replied. "For an experienced project manager, the process of progressive elaboration is welcome. It fills in the holes where we don't fully understand our project and fleshes out our understanding of the solution as we're building it."

The QA analyst hesitated. He was not totally comfortable addressing another project management professional's capabilities beyond the constructive criticism he had included in his carefully worded QA reports.

"In the case of this project manager, I believe the schedule was the project manager's undoing. I believe she constructed the project's schedule at the beginning of the project in earnest, with solid input from her team members. But she neglected to adapt that schedule over time, as the project unfolded. I believe she felt that she and her team could fully understand 100 percent of what was required for their project on day one, not recognizing that every project contains some unknowns that make a hard-and-fast prediction impossible."

"An experienced project manager will facilitate a project team's estimate for a project to the level of detail necessary to understand the work and provide clarity to the team members who will do that work," he continued. "Then that project manager will generally manage the project's efforts at a higher level. We call it the 8/80 rule: Plan to the 8-hour level and manage at the 80-hour level. That provides the team some flexibility to adapt the work as the situation demands. It allows the high-level estimates of project effort and duration to stand on their own even if the detailed estimates flex and morph over time. To be successful, most project managers understand that some flexibility is required for a project schedule to be a useful tool."

"The PM didn't do that, I gather," the CIO concluded.

"Right. Once the schedule was finalized, she believed it to be etched in concrete. She guided the team to the rigid detail level of the schedule they had built. She came absolutely unglued on one occasion when a team member reported that a task was going to take longer than anticipated, even though that task's products would accelerate several other tasks along the project's critical path. The project manager would not accept that input, even yelling at the team member in a meeting—refusing to consider that his innovative approach would have saved the project a week or two of schedule."

The CIO grimaced. "That rigid, huh?"

"Sorry to say, yes. The vendor on the project, who provided several key pieces of analysis for the feasibility study, threatened to quit if the project manager didn't lighten up and exercise a reasonable level of flexibility and understanding. I talked the vendor into staying on the project, but nearly handed in my own resignation when the project manager started yelling at me about how the vendor was not sticking exactly to the project schedule. The vendor was late on a couple of items, true, but none of them were on the project's critical path."

"She actually yelled at you?"

"Yes; I didn't put that in my report. In one of my QA reports, though, I did suggest that the project manager and her team rework a critical element of the risk analysis based on the potential lack of critical data, which would not be made available by an external agency for at least two weeks after the scheduled date. The project manager became irate about the time it would take to do the risk analysis. Her schedule was fixed in place and unmovable. She was willing to live and die by that schedule and expected everyone on the team to do the same, despite situations that arose at various times throughout the project. You may recall that you required the project manager to go back and rework those risks anyway, and it cost the team nearly two weeks of effort."

"I do," the CIO replied. "So, what do you think? Should I use her as a project manager in the future?"

"That sort of recommendation is way outside the scope of my contract as your external QA analyst. That said, I will tell you this: Projects are about people doing work. A schedule is a tool, a guide—and only a guide. By definition, a project of any kind is about producing a unique product, service, or result. That very uniqueness suggests a degree of unknown that cannot be built into a project's schedule on the first day. The best of schedules must include some flexibility and must be able to accommodate change as the unknown becomes known and is built into the project. Without allowing for progressive elaboration, a project is late the day it starts. A good project manager understands this, builds in the contingency, and then manage the team's effort with that understanding."

"Our project manager didn't do that, and she verbally abused anyone who suggested that a change to the schedule might be warranted," the CIO concluded.

"Sadly, that's about the size of it. It's a wonder the team didn't quit in the middle of things," the QA analyst concluded. "It's all a matter of what you want out of your projects. This one was eventually delivered. It was late, in my estimation, because of the project manager's inflexibility and apparent belief that the project schedule is the end-all and be-all of project management. If you want your projects delivered on schedule, with high team morale, then the schedule can't be carved in stone on day one and it must allow for the natural ebb and flow that comes with good project management."

"Thank you," the CIO said. "I think I have my answer."

> **Lesson Learned**
>
> *For the project manager:* Projects are about people doing work. The schedule is just a guide for that work. Manage the people first and above all else for a successful project.

# HUMAN RESOURCE MANAGEMENT

# 9

## Build a Realistic Project Team

The project sponsor welcomed the new project manager into his office. His smile was broad and sincere. "Have a seat, please," he offered. "We're happy to have you on board for our project."

"I'm excited to be here," she replied. "And I'm excited to get started."

"That's great," the project sponsor continued. We are all very excited about the new training project and about your experience managing projects of this type. Your project team is standing by in the conference room, ready to meet you."

The project manager smiled. She had operated as a one-person project management consulting shop and was accustomed to arriving on sites where project teams had already been formed. "I look forward to meeting them. The training program you've hired me to deliver is a complex one, reflecting your new business offerings and the need to deliver distance learning around the globe. The specific skill sets of the team members will be very important in terms of what they bring to the task."

The manager showed the first signs of stress as he replied. "I didn't have a lot of people to choose from. Most of our key resources are involved in setting up new business processes and making connections with our affiliates in Europe and Asia. I did the best I can."

"The short timeline—six months—and the technical demands of this project are significant..." the project manager started. The project sponsor cut off her words as he rose from his desk.

"Let's go meet the team and you can form your own opinion. I'll warn you, though, that we have no one else to give you. You are going to have to make do with who you have."

The project manager followed the sponsor down a long hallway. As they approached the conference room, she heard voices that didn't all sound welcoming.

The sponsor introduced the project manager to the six members of her team and then exited abruptly, begging off to attend another meeting. Once he had left, the project manager invited the team to take seats around the conference table.

"Let's take inventory," she began. "The training project before us involves documenting a new and complex business process; building a curriculum for training front-line salespeople, customer support people, and back office support staff in those processes; creating user manuals and customer interaction guides, site-training tools, and online training tools; and ultimately delivering the training to the company's employees here and around the world. By a show of hands, how many of you have experience with online training?"

No hands went up.

"How many of you have experience developing training curricula?"

Again, no hands. The project manager began to feel her heart sink.

"How many of you have done any training manual development?"

One person raised his hand. "I used to edit textbooks and training manuals for a large publishing house."

The project manager smiled. "That's a good start. Now, who in this group has done any training at all in the past?"

Two more people raised their hands. One was a retired sergeant who had done training in the Army and the other had been a schoolteacher working for a large nonprofit organization teaching in developing countries.

"That's a help," the project manager said. "Let's get an idea of what each of you brings to the project. Please summarize your background and qualifications and I'll take notes."

When she was done, she had recorded the following:

- Sarah was an administrative assistant to one of the organization's high-level managers. She had excellent organizational skills and was adept at preparing documents with many different office software products.
- Bill previously worked as an editor for a large publishing house that specialized in academic texts. He described himself as an introverted lover of words.
- Sam previously worked as a customer service representative for the company, with 15 years of experience under his belt. He liked working with people and possessed a keen understanding of the organization's capabilities and limitations.
- Jean worked in administrative support, sorting and delivering mail, and was concerned that she was not qualified to be on the team. She was seeking to move into a more interesting field, though. She volunteered to take on any task the project manager needed doing, no matter how small or how large.
- Elliot was a retired drill sergeant. His Army career included training young soldiers and problem-solving with them to ensure their success in the military. He had a master's degree in cultural anthropology.

- Shelly had recently transferred from a local school district, changing careers for one she hoped would be less stressful and provide better pay.

The project manager thanked each member of the team for their information and then briefly described the project. She worried that her team lacked the skill sets necessary to develop and deliver a complex training program around the globe using traditional, classroom, and online training techniques, in a number of languages and in a short period of time.

After the meeting, she made her way back to the project sponsor's office and found him digging through a pile of paperwork. "How did the meeting go?" he asked as she took a seat.

"Very nice people," she replied. "I found them to be highly motivated and upbeat. I do worry that they lack the skill sets necessary to deliver this job. I may need to call on you for additional resources."

The business manager frowned. "I am the project sponsor for this effort. I can make decisions that stick and write checks, and I can tell you now that the well is dry. As I said, you need to do the best you can with who you've got. We hired you because of your sterling reputation and are happy to pay your fee, but you must deliver this project with the resources you have."

It was obvious from his tone that the business manager was not going to budge on this issue. For the moment, the project manager decided to let the issue slide. Perhaps there was a way to lay out her case that would help him appreciate the situation better, but now was clearly not the time.

The business manager showed her to a comfortable, windowed cubicle where she set up her laptop and wasted no time getting to work. Using a template from a similar project and some background materials provided by the business manager, she laid out the tasks involved in completing the project, including designing the curriculum, developing a training program, developing and publishing training materials and manuals, establishing web-based training, and creating post-training survey tools.

She then detailed each task involved in developing the project's deliverables, estimating their duration based on her own recent experience. From that, she built a schedule that assumed her team had the necessary skill sets to complete the tasks. Based on her estimates, a skilled team could deliver the project in the six months available, but just barely.

When she was done, she summarized the tasks required to complete the project, walking through the project step by step. She developed a list of the specific skill sets needed to complete the project:

- A production resource skilled at generating computerized presentations and publication-ready documentation. The administrative assistant could handle that job, she was sure, perhaps aided by the highly motivated mailroom clerk.

- A curriculum and training program development lead. This was a role she felt well qualified to fill personally.

- Three instructors for local training. The drill sergeant and the retired teacher might be able to fill two of those slots; if need be, she could take on the remaining task.

- Editing, proofing, and production of training materials. She felt certain Bill would be able to meet this need.

- Subject matter expertise, specifically a business analyst who could interview employees, gather their unique concerns about the new business model, and convert the information to something the team could work with. With his customer service background and long history with the company, Sam would be just the person for the job. She might need to mentor him a bit in generating documentation that she and the others could use for the training program and materials.

- Web-based training development lead. This highly technical individual would need a solid background in internet-based training. None of those on her team possessed those skills; she knew that without them, the project was likely to flounder.

Two days passed before the project manager was able to wrangle an appointment with the project sponsor. As she entered his office, she got the sense that he was not happy to see her.

"What's the problem?" he asked, without inviting her to take a seat.

She did so anyway and began. "During our last meeting, I mentioned my concerns about the makeup of my project team. I've done an analysis of the skill sets needed to complete this project, and I'm short a critical resource. I need someone experienced in web-based training design. It's a technical position and none of my team members has that expertise."

"What about you?" he demanded.

"I do not. That was clear on my resume and in my proposal for this job," she replied.

"Well, just do the best you can. I'll try to get someone from our IT department to help you out," he replied, and began shuffling through a pile of paperwork, effectively dismissing her.

"I really need that resource," she countered. "And it's more than simple software development. Web-based training development is a skill set in and of itself. It requires a high level of sophistication and training."

"Do the best you can," he replied. "I'll see if I can get you a software developer we can spare from our IT shop. I'll let you know."

Back at her office, the project manager adjusted the project schedule to push the web-based training development tasks out

*Chapter 9* ■ *Human Resource Management: Build a Realistic Project Team*

in time as much as possible. Nervous about the impact of that shift, she annotated the risk of not having that skill set on the team in her risk management log and appended it to her project status report, which was due the next day. The report came back from her sponsor with a note that said, "You will have your software guy in two weeks."

Time passed, and both the curricula and the training materials were coming along well. The team turned out to be a highly motivated, positive, collaborative group. Where one team member lacked the skills or experience to get a job done, others would step in and fill the void. The project manager found herself enjoying the camaraderie the team shared and reveled in their progress.

After four months, the web developer still had not shown up, despite the project sponsor's repeated promises and the project manager's reporting the risks in her biweekly project status reports. In her risk management log, she projected at least a 30-day delay in delivering the web-based training to the company's locations in Europe and Asia.

Two weeks later, she was summoned to the project sponsor's office, only to find someone new sitting at the desk. The new person greeted the project manager warmly.

"I have read your last three project status reports with some interest. I recently replaced the person who was in this job before me. He was let go because most of the projects developed to deliver the company's new line of products have fallen on tough times. It appears that he was not listening to his project managers and supporting their needs, as was apparently the case with your project. I believe that you have some unmet needs. Perhaps I can help."

"I do," the project manager responded. She briefly reiterated her need for a skilled web-based training development resource, detailing the work she had done to identify that need.

"That's a good skill set gap analysis," the new project sponsor concluded. "Nice work."

The project sponsor handed the project manager three resumes to review. "I believe these individuals may meet your needs. They are all contractors, like yourself, but we are willing to spend the money to ensure that your training project—and our larger initiative—are successful. Why don't you review those and give me your recommendation. I'll see about expediting the contract and getting your selected person on the job right away."

The project manager let out a sigh of relief. "I can't thank you enough."

"No thanks required. It's what we should have done in the first place. You did a good job on the skill set gap analysis you provided to my predecessor. He should have listened to you then. If I get you this resource, do you think you can pick up some of the schedule delay you projected in your last report?"

"I'll give it a good try," the project manager replied.

Two months later, and only two weeks behind the original schedule, the training project was completed. Reviews by those who received the training exceeded expectations. The entire project team, including the project sponsor, cheered as the project manager wrapped up the last training session on the web, delivered in Spanish, and officially closed the project down.

"Nice job, everyone," the project sponsor exclaimed. "I hope that all of you who participated in this project will consider working in our new training department. It seems like we have a need for that sort of thing around her, based on what we learned from your project."

The project sponsor turned to the project manager and contract web-based training developer. "You two will see a nice bonus in your final checks. I hope you'll both consider working with us on future projects."

Chapter 9 ■ Human Resource Management: Build a Realistic Project Team

Everyone in the room gave a round of applause for a project well done.

> **Lessons Learned**
>
> *For the project manager:* Never accept dictated team membership. Conduct a skill set gap analysis to determine your project team needs. Identify your team requirements from a position of knowledge and ensure you have the resources necessary to get the job done correctly.
>
> *For the project sponsor:* Assigning members to a project team before the project has been defined creates great risk. Those assigned too soon in the process, before project requirements and tasks are defined, may not fill the need.

# Cost Management     10

## Never Lose Track of the Money

The project team left the project closeout meeting with the client in high spirits. The project had come in on schedule and on budget, and had even won some awards. For a small project of its kind, with a budget of just under $1.5 million, the effort had seemed over nearly as soon as it had started for the nine team members.

The group agreed to meet to celebrate at a local watering hole not far from the consulting firm's main office. As the project manager reached for her coat, the project sponsor, a partner at the firm and the project manager's long-time mentor and friend, congratulated her. "Nice project," the sponsor said. It was obvious he had good news to share.

The project manager chuckled as she slipped into her jacket and slung her laptop bag across her shoulders. "It looks like you've swallowed the proverbial canary. Give it up," she prompted.

"Your client just called. They have another $1.1 million to spend, and they'd like you and your team to start back up as soon as you're ready. It's another project like the one you just finished—lots of technology and business processes that need to be shepherded to a new opportunity for the organization."

The last project had been so intense that the project manager had planned a few days off to re-energize. The last project worked out well, but the effort had proved daunting.

"That's a great opportunity," she remarked. "Today's Thursday. I'll get the team back together right after the weekend, if that will work for you. They all could use a little rest and relaxation."

The project sponsor waved toward the door. "You'd better hurry if you want to catch them. I think they have a head start on the way to the pub."

As the project manager turned to leave, the project sponsor added, "And you get one or two for yourself. The management team has decided to let Karl be the project manager on this next job."

"Karl? As in Karl the newly promoted principal in the company? Karl could not manage his way out of a paper bag."

The project sponsor arched an eyebrow but otherwise failed to acknowledge her comment. "He will have you to guide him. I want you to handle customer relations on the project and provide some oversight."

"But he's a principal and I'm just a lowly consultant; a mere employee...."

The project sponsor laughed. "You're a very capable lowly employee, so I'm sure we will be fine."

The weekend passed and the project manager found Karl waiting outside her office as she arrived on Monday morning. He glanced at his watch. "It's already nine, Sarah. Where have you been? We have a project to deliver."

Sarah groaned. "Thanks for the reminder, Karl. Let's meet in the conference room and I'll show you my notes on the new project. A couple of months ago, I helped the client lay out an approach and estimate. It should give you a good start on the planning."

Karl shrugged off her suggestion. "I've reviewed all the data on the client and that last project you did for them. Nice job, by the way."

"Thanks," she replied, powering up her laptop. She did not like where this conversation appeared to be headed. Karl carried some serious baggage from a recent project that had nearly failed. He and his team had not spent adequate time documenting requirements and the project had quickly turned into a disaster.

"I spent a lot of time poring over your notes," Karl started. "I believe that what the client wants is a very complex system, with a lot of variables accounted for in the user screens as well as in how the system runs its calculations."

Sarah disagreed. "You're missing the point. The client views the current system as overly complex, with a lot of functionality they never use."

"I'll be the judge of that," Karl replied. "Clients never know what they want until they get a taste of a good, modernized solution. I'm going to hit them with a major requirements development effort and dazzle them with our attention to detail. There won't be a 'what if' scenario that their new information management system won't be able to handle. And we'll develop the slickest ad hoc reporting capability they have ever seen."

"But I think...."

Karl cut Sarah off and dropped his expression so that he was looking down at her. "I'm the principal on this engagement, Sarah. You are a consultant. Management has given me this project. Your role is to keep the client happy while I deliver the goods. It's obvious that we have different perspectives about this project, so why don't you just stay out of the way while I deliver exactly what they want?"

The project work plan Karl laid out was 12 months long and provided a prototype of the new system for customer review after four months. Sarah had to admit that it was an aggressive approach. She admired the Spartan feel of the schedule while noting that enough detail was provided to give the client confidence that the project could be completed on time. Over the next two months, she watched Karl hold workshop after workshop with the client's staff, documenting requirements in infinite detail.

It was at month four when the client approached Sarah, asking when they might see their first project status report from Karl and whether the pilot system would be available in two more months. "We like Karl's style," the client's business team leader admitted. "But we are getting weary of yet another eight-hour requirements workshop and wonder when we might see visible signs of progress."

Sarah confronted Karl the next morning before the client arrived at the office. "They're worried," she noted, relating her conversation with the client. "They want to know when you're going to show them something they can touch and test, and when they might see a project status report."

"We don't need a project status report right now," Karl replied. "We're deep into the requirements phase of the project. They know that. They're with me every day. What would I put in the project status report beside that we're getting closer every day to having the information we need to build their new system?

"Aren't you worried about the money for the project?" asked Sarah. "You have my team with the client for eight hours a day. You have been burning budget every day and you have no software written."

He waved off her comment. "You worry too much about the little things. If we don't get the requirements nailed down, we won't have to worry about project status reports or project budgets."

Sarah persisted. "Have you considered using rolling-wave planning or maybe an iterative approach? You could build a piece of the new system, deliver it, learn from the effort, and refine the requirement in chunks. The client would see visible signs of progress and be assured that they are getting something for their money."

# Chapter 10 ■ Cost Management: Never Lose Track of the Money

"You worry too much. You just keep the client happy. I'll take care of the project."

"I worry," Sarah responded, "when I see the number of hours you have expended against the contract, all for refining the project's requirements—requirements that could have been developed for different areas of the new system while you had the team writing code and developing the database for the rest of the system."

"You are getting out of line, Sarah. I have a handle on the project. It's mine to manage as I see fit. I'm the project manager and you are an outside consultant. Leave it alone," Karl insisted.

Sarah persisted, legitimately worried, she felt, about the client's perception of the project. "Could you at least send them a project status report? The client caught me in the hall and indicated that he hadn't seen one since the project started."

Karl's expression turned thoughtful. "I suppose a quick status report might not hurt. I could show how much progress we've made in developing our understanding of the project."

Sarah smiled. "I think that will go a long ways toward gaining the client's confidence."

Two hours later, Karl burst into Sarah's office, holding a single sheet of paper in his hand. "This is a disaster," he proclaimed. "We have a problem."

"What's the problem?" she asked.

"We're out of money," he replied.

Sarah reached for the project status report. At the bottom of the report, below the long section describing what had been accomplished on the project, and just after the shorter list of what was planned for the next few weeks, was a summary of the project's financial status. She read the numbers aloud. "You have spent $960,000 of the $1.1 million budget?"

Karl nodded. "I didn't realize that we had burned so many hours on the requirements."

Sarah shook her head slowly. "You have nearly exhausted the budget on a software development project and your team has not written a single line of code."

"What are we going to do?" Karl asked.

Sarah laid the report on her desk. "What's this 'we' you are using? I seem to recall your advising me pretty specifically about my role on the project. It's your project. You're the principal of the company, in charge of this effort, and you are going to have to tell the client—and our management team—right away."

"But what can I do to recover?"

"It's a little late for that now, isn't it? As for me, I'm going to brush up my resume. I believe our firm is about to get a black eye that it will be difficult to recover from."

The next day, Karl briefed the client about the funding issue. By the time Karl returned to his office, there was an email announcing that the client had fired the firm from the project. Karl was invited to the boardroom to meet with the management team.

Sarah saw Karl in the hallway as he headed to meet with the management team. She felt a little bad for him, noting his hang-dog expression. That was the last time she saw Karl at the company. Then and there, she resolved that if she found herself in the role of project manager, no matter what size project she worked on, she would always be sure she knew the financial status of her team's efforts.

> **Lesson Learned**
>
> *For the project manager:* Always know the financial status of your project. Money flies quickly in the thick of a project's efforts and can disappear before you know it.

# PROJECT GOVERNANCE

## 11

# Organizational Support Is a Key Success Factor

Glenn Briskin, PMP

Lots of the project success (and failure) factors we hear about—executive sponsor support, user involvement, clear business objectives and requirements—can be completely dependent on support from the organization that is beyond the control of the project manager. You may assume you have that support or the project wouldn't be happening. But you do so at your peril.

A large health services company had grown rapidly, building a beautiful new 15-story building to house all its employees. The company was doing so well that it needed to expand its location further.

The company bought a building across the street and planned to move several of its publishing groups into a consolidated group that would share the massive copiers and printers as well as the skilled people required to publish its products. The project involved preparing the building, re-engineering the publishing processes, helping build a new publishing organization, expanding the IT infrastructure to the new building, and completing the transition smoothly so that clients continued to get their publications.

The IT director who hired the project manager was nervous about owning this project. The first words out of his mouth were "Nobody wants to do this." The different divisions in the company that had always produced their own publications liked having their own people and processes. No one wanted to work outside the beautiful new building. It seemed to him that there were so many risks—so much that could go wrong—that his expectation for the project manager was just to get through this without screwing up too much.

Fortunately, the project manager found and focused on a few project support factors that were critical to the project's success. When you are new to a project, your initial impressions can stimulate clear insights. In this case, the project manager thought about the "nobody wants to do this" comment and wondered what could motivate the hundreds of people involved to want to do this. How were all these people who didn't really see themselves as part of the project going to have the same vision for its outcomes, make the time needed to implement the changes, and support it until it delivered on the benefits expected?

The project team figured out that about 200 stakeholders within the company were involved in the publishing processes. It seemed that most of these people didn't want to see this project happen. The project team would have to work with them to understand their processes, find new ways to carry out those processes, and motivate the stakeholders to get on board.

The project team began by identifying a few motivated early adopters and working with them to understand old processes and start defining new ones. The company was just starting casual Fridays, so the project manager approached human resources with an idea for garnering visibility for the project and recognizing early adopters. HR gave the okay to design and distribute t-shirts provided they incorporated the correct logo and colors. The project team decided to print "We're On the Move" with the logo and the new building address on the shirts.

Fifty shirts came in and the next Friday a dozen people were wearing them. The project manager's phone rang off the hook with "How do I get one of those shirts?" "Well, you have to be

*Chapter 11* ■ *Project Governance: Organizational Support Is a Key Success Factor*

on the project." "How do I get on the project?" "If you are part of the publishing process, we have to get your unit together, map out the current process, and put together a new one." "I'm in; make an appointment."

The 50 t-shirts went fast and another 100 were ordered. The project team got HR to let people wear the t-shirts any day of the week. The t-shirts alone didn't turn the stakeholders from "don't want to" to "want to," but it was a start. It turned out that getting people to "want to" took a 30-second speech from the company's chairman.

The team leads—the IT lead, the facilities lead, and the project manager—made an appointment with the company's chairman and primary owner to talk about the new building. The chairman wanted to ensure that the work on the new building would properly reflect the company's position in the city. They talked about the building renovation, foot traffic between the buildings, and the project's progress. The team leads gave the chairman a t-shirt and said that they were working on getting everyone's support. They explained that they needed numerous individuals to buy into the project, understand the changes to production processes, and support their efforts. The chairman said he would give it some thought.

A couple of weeks later, and just a week before the project went live, the company held its annual meeting for employees. Everyone boarded buses to a local theater and watched a slide show featuring company and employee accomplishments. At one point, the chairman reached into a bag and pulled out a "We're On the Move" t-shirt. In about 30 seconds he explained that everyone wearing the t-shirt was a pioneer for the company's future. The company had to expand beyond its headquarters to grow and prosper. People needed to accept the changes involved and help the move succeed. He made it clear that he appreciated the employees' pioneering spirit.

The chairman's 30-second speech made the t-shirt a symbol of the company's future. The project team had a vision everyone could share. They ordered lots more t-shirts and got everyone to wear them on go-live day. The company had gone from "nobody wants to do this" to "everyone wants to be part of it."

The project team had fulfilled the project support factors necessary to make the project a success. While everything didn't go perfectly in the first weeks, everyone did their best to make the project work, and it did. The project manager was assigned another project with the company, and the team got an award from the company later in the year for "the move."

In my consulting work, I often have to evaluate a project that is just starting up or is in flight. My evaluation model includes these specific project support factors:

- Clear shared vision of the project's outcome and expected benefits that is expressed consistently by the organization's leaders
- Governance that is empowered by the organization to provide timely, flexible, and consistent decision-making in support of the project
- Organizational capacity that is sufficient to support the work of the project in view of its regular work and the other projects underway
- Organizational synergy that is characterized by all parts of the organization working together to support the project
- Sustainability considered in the project's scope of work so that the outcome supports delivering benefits for the full expected life
- Business and technical skills that are sufficient to support the change expected by the organization and management of the people and vendors involved.

The biggest factor in this project's success was finding and acting on the unmet project support factors. The project team members didn't assume they had the organization's support, that everyone shared a vision of the project that made it important to the organization, or that people would support the project by

*Chapter 11* ■ *Project Governance: Organizational Support Is a Key Success Factor*

changing their work and stick with it until the changes brought about the required outcomes. Instead of asking people to change a process and move to a new building, the team asked them to take a step toward the organization's future. The team found a way to connect to the organization and got its support.

> **Lesson Learned**
>
> *For the project manager:* Never assume that a project is supported by the organization. Seek a shared vision and validate its importance to the project as well as to the organization's future to ensure organizational buy-in and project success.

# Project Initiation  12

## The Charter Is the First, Best Tool for Project Clarity

The project sponsor had been working in his job for a very long time. He managed a huge piece of a state health and human services agency and desperately needed to streamline business processes, get his staff up to speed with the changing landscape of healthcare regulation, and introduce new and improved automated systems. He hired one of the nation's most respected consulting companies to develop and run the project, but after 10 months of effort, the project was making no apparent progress.

Through the course of those 10 months, massive quantities of consulting fees flew from his budget. People worked constantly, diligently gathering information, learning, writing white papers, and publishing reports. The place was a flurry of activity, yet nothing had been produced that moved the project forward.

In desperation, the project sponsor called a woman he had known professionally for a long time, who specialized in projects of this kind. "Jane," he started, "this is William, over at State. I need your help."

Jane laughed. "Well, that's a fine howdy-do. You must have a problem, not even asking how I'm doing before you ask me for assistance."

"We're in trouble over here," he replied, explaining his situation.

"I understand," Jane responded. "I think we can work this out for you. I'll have my agency send along some contracts for you all to sign. In the meantime, why don't you send me your project management–related documents?"

"You don't know what you're asking for," he replied. "I'm awash in paperwork, reports, and analyses. It would take you months to wade through all this stuff."

"Just send me the project management documents you have. I'd like to start there," she replied.

"Can you give me a clue? What are you looking for?"

"If you see a project plan, a communications plan, or a project management plan, just send it along," she replied.

"I think I have some of those somewhere. I'll see what I can find and send them to you. Could you take a look at them and then meet with me?" he asked.

"How soon do you need to see me?" she asked.

"This afternoon?"

"You are in trouble, aren't you? I'll drop by around 3:00 pm, if you can get me those documents by 10:00 this morning," Jane responded.

When Jane showed up in William's office that afternoon, she held a thin document that William had sent her, labeled a project charter. Her briefcase included a second, massive document: a project schedule. She set the charter on her lap but left the 50-page schedule in her briefcase. "I think I can see your problem, she said."

William smiled. "That's good news. That means we can fix it."

Jane nodded. "I think so. The main issue here is that after reading your project charter, I still have no idea what it is you want out of the project. You say you have white papers about the

# Chapter 12 ■ Project Initiation: The Charter Is the First, Best Tool for Project Clarity

nation's and the state's new healthcare reforms, and that you are overloaded with reports and other documents developed by your staff and the consulting group you hired for this project. You have a massive, expensive project schedule that goes on for several years. But through all that, I see nothing about what you expect to have when the project is done."

William gestured toward a bookcase stacked high with printed documents. "The project team has done all this work."

Jane persisted. "But what, exactly, are they writing all of those for? They may contain hugely valuable information, but until you, as the project sponsor and owner of this effort, define what it is this project is to provide, they cannot be sure of their direction and you cannot be sure that their efforts are worth the cost."

William leaned back heavily in his chair. "I'm beginning to see your point."

"We have a saying in project management that goes something like this: 'If you can see it, we can build it. But if you can't see it, we're not going anywhere.' You can't expect your consulting firm or your staff, no matter how much you pay them or how many people you put on the project, to give you anything meaningful unless you give them a clear picture of what you want from their work."

"But I told them what I want. I need an informed, trained staff, lean business processes, and the infrastructure required to run this agency."

Jane shook her head. "That's a good start, but frankly, without a bit more clarity, it's a lot of fluff. Think about it for a minute. What does each of those things mean? How do you know if and when you have an informed staff? How do you know when they are where you need them? What types of business processes need re-engineering to make your organization leaner? Which ones specifically? And what do you mean by infrastructure? Do you need a new, enterprisewide IT system, or some new phones and desktop computers?"

She continued. "This project charter provides little direction for your project team. I am not surprised you are feeling frustrated. Without direction from you, it's unlikely your team will be headed anywhere meaningful, unless by sheer accident."

Jane took out a piece of legal paper and a pen. "Let's do a little exercise."

William looked at his watch. "I have another meeting at 4:00. Can we get this done by then?"

Jane smiled. "This will be the most worthwhile 45 minutes of your week. We will redirect your project and get it on track for success."

Jane opened the project charter. "First, and foremost, there is no problem statement in this document that says why this project should be done. Let's see if we can flesh one out."

William brightened. "I have a white paper here that identifies the changes in healthcare legislation for the state. Let's begin by targeting that."

Jane nodded. "That's a good start. I'll work that into a business case if you feel strongly that the paper defines the changes in legislation your organization needs to address. How about the business processes that you want made 'lean' ?"

William handed her another document that the consulting firm had prepared describing the agency's business processes. "This report lays out our business architecture," he explained. It defines 20 business processes, noting their relationship to our agency's business objectives. Of those, at least five will need to be reconstructed and defined to sync with our legislative mandates."

Jane put the report in her briefcase. "That will go a long way toward defining your vision for the project. It will tell me how things will be different once the project is completed, who will be impacted by the project, and perhaps even the value you hope to gain from the project. That will be an excellent start

Chapter 12 ◼ Project Initiation: The Charter Is the First, Best Tool for Project Clarity

on the vision statement. What about those changes to the infrastructure?"

"The systems we use are largely manual," William responded. "The business processes identified in that report need to be automated and integrated with federal and other state agencies. Integrating them will enable our staff to serve those who depend on us for their health and wellness more effectively."

"Now, what about your project's budget, team structure, risks that might affect the project, and what should be included in the scope of this effort?" Jane asked.

"The budget is easy," said William. "That's well defined, although I am worried about the rate at which the consultants are burning hours. The consultants and my staff are spending time in some areas where I don't think we are ready to go. I can list those for you. As for risks, I have been worried silly about this project. If we don't get it right, not only will we be in very hot water with the feds and the governor's office, but we'll be risking penalties from civil lawsuits."

"Send me what you have and I'll see what I can do about getting you a good starting point for reorienting this project," Jane replied. "Can you provide me your documents by noon tomorrow? I'll meet with you the following day."

"Absolutely," William said. "Anything you can do will be appreciated. You really think you can help with this?"

Jane smiled. "I know I can."

Jane returned two days later with a new project charter in hand. She laid the voluminous project schedule on William's desk; it was apparent from the first page that she had taken a red pen and worked the schedule over extensively.

"This new project charter contains what you need to get your project back on course. I am sure that your consulting firm and staff will be pleased to get your guidance, assuming, of course, that you agree with what I have documented in the charter. Why don't you take a few minutes to look through it now?"

William opened the document, which was about 40 pages long. The table of contents made a lot of sense:

1. Vision Statement
2. Business Problem, Need, or Opportunity
3. Project Objectives
4. Description of the Product to be Produced
5. High-Level Schedule/Milestones
6. Project Governance
7. Roles and Responsibilities
8. Assumptions and Constraints
9. Major Deliverables
10. High-Level Risks
11. Budget and Budget Management
12. Project Charter Approval Form
13. Appendix – High-Level Scope Statement.

William scanned each section of the project charter and was impressed. "This document," he said, "lays things out pretty clearly. The vision and objectives provide the project team, including the consultants, specific direction. The scope statement presents important information and the rest of the document provides key boundaries for the team. I want to look over the governance section a bit to make sure it syncs with my own management style and inclinations, but this is an excellent document. I can see what you meant when you implied that if I had a good vision of where things needed to go, the team's efforts would benefit. Why didn't I do this before?"

Jane responded, "The proof of what you are seeing is in the markup I did of your project's schedule. I simply struck through

## Chapter 12 ■ Project Initiation: The Charter Is the First, Best Tool for Project Clarity

any work or requirements that did not directly support your vision statement, or that went outside the boundaries set by your scope statement. Based on that, I believe that you can knock six months off the schedule. I'd want to do a deeper review of the schedule before drawing any final conclusions, but it looks to me like you can get your people trained and up to speed, then have them assist with the business process re-engineering, and bring on a software integrator to help you select and customize a software solution to support your business needs."

"It's that clear?" William asked.

"I can see this project at its end, its successful end," Jane continued. "You'll need a more defined planning document, what we call a project plan, to augment what we have in the charter, but yes, I believe this project can be successful if you can bring on a project manager to execute your vision and objectives and to deliver your scope. With what you have here, I can see someone pulling this together successfully in a relatively short period of time."

William smiled. "Just scanning this project charter, I get a clearer picture of how things might work out for the project and the agency. Three days ago, I was frustrated and depressed. Now, with this charter, I can see success."

"In the future," Jane replied, "always start with a good project charter. That's the way to initiate a project. It takes a month or so to put together a good charter, and it will be worth its weight in gold to the project. The charter establishes a solid starting point for a project and will help you, as the project sponsor, decide if you should do the project at all."

"Thanks, Jane," William said. "This was a great few days. Any chance I could talk you into being the project manager for this project?"

Jane smiled again. "You already have one of those. And besides, I only take on projects where management is willing to adopt a good project management methodology and invest in doing the effort right."

William held up the new project charter. "I'm a believer."

"Then maybe next time you should call me to be your project manager," Jane replied.

> **Lesson Learned**
>
> *For the project sponsor:* Clarity is essential. Achieving clarity in the project charter greatly enhances the likelihood of your project delivering what you need.

# PROCUREMENT MANAGEMENT

# 13

## Take the Time Necessary to Ensure Project Success

Gary Hudson, PMP

One of our project's objectives was to acquire a commercial off-the-shelf (COTS) software product to support a business area's critical needs. Although the organization had experience with this type of work, the individual team members didn't know exactly what they needed to do. Our project sponsor picked a date about six months out as the target for publication of the request for proposals (RFP) and we set about organizing for that milestone.

We kicked off the project by gathering business requirements through workshops with a representative group of users. Work processes were identified and used to elicit the underlying requirements.

We captured the requirements in a spreadsheet to facilitate sorting and filtering. Following the business requirements sessions, we analyzed and scrutinized the requirements to provide consistency in level of detail and completeness. We also worked with technical staff to identify the technical and non-functional requirements. We then shared the restructured and reorganized requirements with the project's stakeholders for review and acceptance.

The challenge with this process was that most users were not accustomed to explaining their work in this fashion and consequently could not be relied on to describe their requirements fully. The business analysts involved also lacked experience gathering the requirements for procurement of a COTS solution. So how could we ensure that the business requirements were adequately documented?

One approach we used to reduce this risk was to employ use cases as a tool for defining project requirements. Each use case described user actions, and computer reactions, in a step-by-step manner. This started with identifying the high-level business process and breaking it down to a use-case level, that is, where a user could comfortably explain its use of the system.

The project team relied on a use-case template to document that process, along with its dependencies, interactions, steps, and business rules. The idea was that we would get the user to imagine using a new system and describe the steps that would be part of completing the process.

Most organizations have used contracts to acquire products and services, and we were no different. Our job was to explain to the contracts specialist exactly what we needed.

We wrestled with the question of how much control the project manager should relinquish to the contracts specialist in developing the contract. Like the project team, the contracts specialist might not have specific experience with a COTS procurement. We believed that in some instances, our contracts specialist exercised too much control over the *what* and the *how* of the contract rather than just advising and guiding the project team. This resulted in too many review and revision cycles in the contract development process, not to mention the team's general frustration.

It became clear to us that the project manager is the customer and the contracts specialist is the advisor when it comes to contracting. The team was forced to rely on the contracts specialist for his expertise in contracts. The contracts specialist was required to integrate with the project team to understand the needs and requirements in the contract and work as a team

## Chapter 13 ■ Procurement Management: Take the Time Necessary to Ensure Project Success

member, under project management direction, to design and develop a contract that meets the project's needs.

Once we had a contract in place, we discovered that the ability to ensure that communications with the vendor flow smoothly depends in large part on how the contract is negotiated and documented. We needed to address a variety of areas from the obvious to the tedious, including contract default, arbitration, amendment, change control, deliverable approval, status reporting, and schedule milestones.

Each of these processes had to be outlined in sufficient detail to ensure common understanding and enforceability with the vendor. These details were ultimately developed through role-playing scenarios where someone played the vendor and we worked through various bad-news scenarios. The key was to anticipate—and document—what might happen under those scenarios.

For instance, we used a deliverable expectation document (DED) to facilitate the vendor communication process. At the beginning of each deliverable, the vendor was required to create a DED that included a table of contents, a sentence or two describing each section, the approach to developing the content, who would be involved, and how we would know when the deliverable was complete.

The DED was prepared, reviewed, and approved before work began on any written deliverable. This process allowed for mutual review and consideration as each deliverable was started, which provided an opportunity to reflect on what might be contained in the document prior to any significant effort to create it. This is turn reduced the number of reviews and revisions required. The DED process made final approval of the deliverable much easier, since expectations on both sides were clear from the beginning.

The performance aspect of the contract can be structured in a number of ways. Our project used a deliverable-based approach. The entire engagement was broken down into phases, with each phase having one or more deliverables. Payment was tied to the completion of each approved deliverable based on pre-agreed acceptance criteria.

In the case of our COTS project, the deliverables included the project management plan, functional requirements specification, technical specification, pilot implementation plan, configuration and customization plan, user acceptance test plan, post-implementation support plan, and year 1 and year 2 production support agreements. These all required extensive development by the vendor. The DED process facilitated a much abbreviated development timeframe for each deliverable.

We also considered numerous approaches to evaluating and selecting a COTS vendor for this project. In our deliberations, we determined that the RFP process must clearly articulate what we needed from the vendors. We put ourselves in the vendor's chair and asked ourselves how the vendor might interpret what we were requesting.

The scoring of vendor proposals presented some challenges and opportunities for us. Determining the right weighting for each element of a proposal is not as straightforward as it might seem. Each area has a multitude of criteria that could be scored; determining how much is sufficient for the purpose at hand proved challenging for our team.

We developed a sensitivity analysis tool and conducted several mock evaluations to test for the optimal outcome. For instance, if a vendor had a product that was great from a business perspective but not such a great fit technically, how did it rank compared to a vendor that offered a more balanced product? Failure to get this part right could have put our evaluation team in the difficult position of having to recommend a product that no one liked.

In the end, we selected a vendor and a software package. In some ways we all felt that better software might be available somewhere on the market, but our successful vendor represented the best blend of people, software, and technical fit for our environment.

In hindsight, we seem to have done some things right but we could have done others better. That said, we ultimately got our project delivered successfully, thanks to the deliberate process we followed and the time that we took to define an effective requirements gathering and procurement process.

> **Lesson Learned**
>
> *For the project manager:* Deliberate, clearly defined processes and expertise are essential for a successful project procurement.

# Project Planning    14

## Those Who Do, Should Plan

The call came in on a Friday, as the project management consultant was heading for the door. He had just celebrated closing out a project and was looking forward to a three-day weekend before figuring out what his next project would be. The previous project had been a long, hard haul and he was ready for some time off before seeking the next challenge.

But his curiosity got the better of him and he took the call. "Project Solutions," he said. "This is Ron. How can I help you?"

He recognized the voice on the line. A few years earlier, Sarah had called him with a particularly tough project. It was halfway through a 12-month schedule, was failing fast, and involved critical elements of her company's business line.

"Good afternoon, Sarah. It's been a while. I assume you're not calling me to wish me a good weekend."

Sarah chuckled. "I could do that, I suppose, but I'm really calling you to see if you might be available to help us with another project. You really pulled our project out of the fire a few years back. Are you interested in picking up a new project?"

Ron glanced at the clock. "I was just headed out for a long weekend, but the beach will still be there later. What have you got?" he asked as he shrugged off his jacket and pulled out his desk chair.

"The project is just under $50 million in value," Sarah replied. "It's heavy in information technology, infrastructure, radio operations, and business process. The outcomes will span the entire state and integrate with federal and local jurisdictions."

"The Federal Communications Commission has mandated a move from broadband radio to narrowband radio to free up bandwidth along the airways. Our organization thinks it would be a good time to convert from analog to digital radio and to interface with local and federal jurisdictions. We plan to piggyback on other agencies' antenna towers and trunking capabilities."

"The bottom line is that the project was scheduled for 18 months and it's now at the end of its second year," she continued. "The FCC has granted an extension against a mandatory timeline, but we are unsure about our ability to get it done on time even with the waiver. Our team of radio and technology specialists has been doing the best they can, as the prime vendor for the project has, but we are a little lost. We feel the project could use project management resuscitation. I know you specialize in revamping troubled project; we could use your help."

"It sounds challenging," Ron replied. "Why don't you send over whatever you've got by way of project schedules, plans, contracts, and so on. I'll take a look at them over the weekend and get back to you on Tuesday."

"I just emailed them to you. Any chance you could get back to me earlier, like Monday morning?" Sarah asked.

Ron opened his email. Sure enough, Sarah had already sent him most of what he'd need to size up the project. "I just completed a really tough project. I need a few days. It'll take me a little time to take a look at this gigabyte of documents you just sent me, anyway. I'm afraid it will be Tuesday."

"Tuesday it is. Thanks, Ron."

Ron saved the files Sarah sent, closed the laptop, grabbed his portable printer, and headed for his car. Three hours later, he

*Chapter 14* ■ *Project Planning: Those Who Do, Should Plan*

found himself in a hotel room with a panoramic view of the Pacific Ocean. The wind was howling outside and the rain was coming down in sheets. Clearly not a beach day. He began to wade through the project charter, schedule, vendor contract, recent project meeting reports, and working group notes.

A report provided by an external quality assurance consultant immediately caught Ron's interest. The consultant suggested that the project schedule was unrealistic, considered only the vendor's tasks, and did not seem to follow a logical path toward project completion. Further, the QA analyst suggested that the project scope was a moving target that, in itself, reduced the project's chances of success.

Ron spent several hours poring over the project's schedule, which appeared to have been updated three times in the past year. Each time the vendor had provided an update, the schedule had slipped another three to five months. By the time Ron finished with the schedule, it was 8:00 in the evening. He sorted through the files and found the project's contact list. He ran down the list until he found the name and number of the person he needed. It was late, he decided, but why not try calling the vendor's project manager now?

Shaun Haskins answered. "Can I help you?"

Ron figured the best approach was the direct one, so he got right to the point. "My name is Ron Felder. Sarah, your project sponsor, has asked me to pick up the radio broadband project. I have just spent several hours with your project artifacts and wondered if you might have a minute for a few questions."

"I don't recognize your name, but you seem to know Sarah. I'm still at the office, so I guess I can take a few minutes," Shaun replied.

"I've worked through a ton of project artifacts and pretty much landed on the project schedule. I keep coming back to it, in fact. I could not help but notice that you seem to be doing the project solo, without any input from Sarah's group. I've also noted in numerous meeting minutes that Sarah's group has an ongoing concern over repeated schedule slips, which generally seem to occur every time you update the schedule for her. Can you fill me in on that?"

Shaun's sigh came through loud and clear. "I know the schedule slips are frustrating for her because they are frustrating for us."

"You provide the schedule, so I would think you have control over how things shake out on the project. What's driving the situation?"

"We make the schedule and have a pretty good idea of what we need to do, but this project leverages a lot of existing infrastructure and that requires a lot of work by Sarah's group," Shaun replied. "Their work is driven by our work and our work is driven by their work. Sometimes work is done independently with interfaces and dependencies between efforts that don't materialize until months down the road. The pressure from the FCC and our client has my management team jumping; they often demand timelines that meet externally imposed time constraints but are not realistic.

"I believe Sarah has experienced the same sort of thing," he continued. "Her management team has influenced the schedule to the extent that it cannot possibly be realistic, placing demands on our team that cannot be met. Sarah's team identifies more and more work as we go through the schedule, expanding the project's scope and adding to the timeline. We keep falling further and further behind."

Ron nodded as he considered Shaun's view, which appeared validated by the schedule, the project's planning documents, and the meeting notes.

"If I can get the go-ahead from Sarah, would you commit to bringing your technical team to a planning session next week? I have an idea that I think could get this project on a track that you, your technical team, your management team, and Sarah's group might appreciate," suggested Ron.

# Chapter 14 ■ Project Planning: Those Who Do, Should Plan

Shaun gave Ron his cell phone number. "Text me the date, time, and location and we'll be there. Give me a day's notice to arrange flights for some of my team."

Ron thanked Shaun for the discussion and then called Sarah at her office. "That was quick," she said as she answered the phone. "What's up?"

Ron related his call with Shaun, adding, "I'll take the project. We can work the contract issues on Tuesday morning, when I get to your office. What I'd really like is for you to book a small conference room at the hotel near your office for next Thursday if possible and invite your technical team. I'll need a day of dedicated time from them. You can attend too, if you like. But as the project sponsor, I'll want you to stay in the background and not actively participate."

Sarah chuckled. "Are you telling me to keep my mouth shut?" She paused, and when he did not respond, she added, "I can do that."

"Thanks," Ron replied. "I'll see you on Tuesday. I'll just need a place to work. I would like to talk to your project team's technical lead on Tuesday or Wednesday at the latest."

"He's a member of your team now," Sarah replied. "I'll let him know that his new boss needs to see him on Tuesday. I'm sure it won't be a problem."

Over the weekend Ron spent more time with the project artifacts, researching the project's vendor online and looking into the FCC's narrowband initiative. By Sunday, the weather cleared and he enjoyed a restful day before he embarked on what he expected would be a very challenging project.

On Tuesday, Ron found himself ensconced in a small office sorting through shared project files on Sarah's organization's network. Shortly after lunch, the project's technical team leader, Larry, showed up at his desk and the two headed to a nearby coffee shop to discuss the project.

Larry had been with Sarah's group for more than 25 years. After a few minutes of talking with him, Ron knew he was totally dedicated to the project's success. The technical lead reiterated much of what Shaun had said on the phone a few days earlier. "Management feels so pressured by the FCC that they push unrealistic timeframes on this project. We know what needs to be done, but everyone's so gun-shy about the schedule that no one wants to raise the main issue."

"And what is the main issue?" Ron asked.

"It's easy, really," Larry replied. "We need to make our schedule more than a vendor's task list. We need to integrate our work with the vendor's work in a single planning document so that we have a comprehensive picture of what it will take to get this project done. Once we've done that, we need to freeze the scope—and get on with the business of getting the job done."

As they walked back to the office together, Ron turned to Larry. "Did Sarah tell you about the meeting with the vendor?"

Larry nodded.

"Good. Have your team there, ready to work, bright and early."

Thursday morning, Sarah's three team members filed into the room, with the vendor's team following. Shaun projected the current project schedule on the room's large screen and Ron kicked things off.

"We have seven hours of time available to us today," he started. "The purpose of this workshop is for you, the people who have to do the work, or who directly supervise those who have to do the work, to replan the project schedule."

A member of the vendor's technical team spoke up. "We know our work and what we need to do. We've tried to fix things in the past, but the scope keeps moving around. Sarah's group keeps adding work to the schedule every few weeks, and we can't seem to move forward."

"I understand," Ron replied. "Sarah has agreed to let us do our work here today without interference from senior management. Your bosses have agreed to the same ground rule. By the end of the day, we need to have an integrated project schedule that includes all the major pieces of work necessary to get the project done. Importantly, that schedule will be built by the people who have to do the work. We need you to lay out the work as carefully, realistically, and in as much detail as possible."

Ron continued. "But that won't be the end of it. Even with all of you building a realistic schedule for this effort, no one can know exactly what will be needed in any project two years down the road. People who believe that are just kidding themselves. Things change. So, to make our schedule work for us, we will use a process called rolling-wave planning."

"Using rolling-wave means that every month, we will meet and detail out the schedule for the next 30 days to refresh it, validate it, and elaborate on it if needed. We will also take a look at the 60 days beyond that and refine that schedule as much as we are able. We will continue this process until the project is done. For today's rescheduling effort, we will do our best to determine the high-level requirements and tasks for the rest of the project. We will build in risk where there's a valid need and trim what we can as long as we are not sacrificing quality."

The team got to work. The discussions were tentative, exploring this new approach to planning the project. Once it became apparent that Sarah and her team were serious about the effort, the vendor's team joined in the planning process enthusiastically. Six hours later, the workshop concluded and Ron presented the schedule to Sarah.

Ron pointed to a line on the screen that said "FCC Compliance." "Here's where you are done," he said. "In our estimate, it will take another 20 months to perform all the work needed to get there. From my research, the FCC has already granted extensions to numerous groups like yours that are behind on their effort to comply with the new rules. Additionally, other groups conducting similar projects have required four years to get the job done. With this schedule extension, that's about where you will be: at four years."

Sarah stood from her chair and faced the group. "Thank you for all the work you've done here today. I have a new appreciation of the complexity of this project and what it will take to get the work done. I also realize the hazards of management's attempting to impose artificial limits on a project of this kind. You've laid out a good plan today. As they say in the project management business, 'It is what it is.' We would be foolish to think we can change that."

Sarah turned to Shaun. "If your management team agrees, we will approve this new schedule for moving forward. I will deal with the FCC. For the rest of you here, thanks for educating me about what it takes to build a real project schedule."

Eighteen months later, the project was completed two months earlier than anticipated due to a change in scope that eliminated several major requirements. As Ron left the project closeout party, he could not help but remember the words he had read so many times when it came to planning a project: "Let those who do the work, plan the project. Management can kid themselves all day long when it comes to project timelines, but no one can kid the worker."

**Lesson Learned**

*For the project manager and the project sponsor:* Let those who do the work, plan the work. Otherwise, the schedule is fabrication, speculation, and too often, fiction.

# RISK MANAGEMENT   15

## Even the Best Planning Does Not Eliminate Risk

The flight simulator was loaded on the flatbed truck in the frigid upstate New York morning air. It was February, and snow covered the ground. The night before, the locks on Dave's garage door and car doors had frozen solid. It had taken a scorched screwdriver and more than one butane lighter to get him on the road to work that morning. Now he stood staring at the long flatbed with $20 million worth of motion systems, computers, simulator body, and F16 avionics. The crates stood a good eight feet above the bed of the truck.

He turned toward Craig, the project manager for the Norway F16 flight simulator project, who smiled and rubbed his hands together. "We've been a year building and testing this simulator. We've shipped more than 20 of them all around the world. I've coordinated the shipment of each and every one of them, and I still get excited and worried about this last piece of the project."

Dave watched as the driver of the truck carefully inspected each of the tie-down straps that held the massive crates in place. He noted the interesting Norwegian labeling marking each crate. "But the project's done," he offered. "You should be celebrating."

Craig gave Dave a sidelong glance and turned away, heading for the warmth of the project office. He called back over his shoulder, "I'll celebrate once they've signed for those crates at the Norwegian Air Force base."

Two days later, Craig showed up at Dave's cubicle with a broad smile on his face. "It's arrived!"

"The simulator?" Dave asked.

"What else?" Craig replied. "They just off-loaded it from the aircraft and are putting it on the flatbed truck that will take it to the air base. You don't know how hard this delivery was to arrange. That truck has to travel all across Norway. Many of the roads there are very narrow, unlike our highways. They frequently wind under overpasses that were built hundreds of years ago. The research I did on the roads was lengthy and challenging. I had to get first-person verification from people on the ground for those overpasses. It took weeks of phone calls, interpreters, and insurance inspectors, but I got it all nailed down. When you deliver something as massive and expensive as one of these simulators, you can't take anything for granted. I'm going to stay in touch with the delivery team by phone each step of the way and plot it on my computer. Want to watch with me?"

Dave had only been with the flight simulator company for six months and found the work to be stimulating. Even so, the prospect of sitting with Craig for the six hours it would take for the simulator to move from the air terminal to the air base was not enticing.

"How about if I check in with you in a couple of hours and then watch as you track it onto the air base?" Dave suggested.

Craig shrugged as he headed back to his office. "Okay, but you'll miss all the fun."

Two hours later, Dave stopped by Craig's office. He noticed the map on the wall with the red push pins marking the simulator's planned route across Norway and the blue pins noting the truck's actual progress. Craig was on the phone, but he gave Dave a thumbs-up, indicating that all was proceeding as planned.

Near the time the simulator was scheduled to arrive at the air base, Dave made his way once again to Craig's office. He

# Chapter 15 ■ Risk Management: Even the Best Planning Does Not Eliminate Risk

noticed a crowd of 10 or 11 people gathered at the door. The F16 flight simulator program director, Vince, was in the group. Everyone was smiling and apparently sharing some sort of joke.

Vince stepped away from the group and met Dave as he approached. Craig moved over to stand beside their mutual boss, looking glum.

"Did it go well?" Dave asked.

Before Craig could respond, Vince chimed in. "Not exactly," he said. "You want to tell him, Craig, or should I? You planned this thing to death. You have annoyed all of us with your enthusiasm and stories of what it took to plan the route from the airport to the base. In fact, I have never seen any delivery plan so complete. It was foolproof."

Vince snickered and began to laugh. He turned away from Craig and Dave and made his way back to the group hanging out by the door to Craig's office. As Vince approached the group, someone pointed into Craig's office and said, "Look at the photos. They are coming up on Craig's computer now."

Those words were followed by a lot of "oohs and ahs" until someone said, "so sad," and everyone but Vince headed back to their offices.

Craig looked at Dave. "You remember how I told you I carefully calculated every step of the route for the delivery of that simulator?"

Dave nodded.

"I knew the width of every road, and I calculated all the necessary detours and side roads to accommodate the truck's height and overpass clearance until I was blue in the face."

Vince let out a guffaw and slapped Craig on the back. "Until we were all blue in the face from hearing you talk about it, you mean. This wouldn't be funny at all if you hadn't been so obnoxious about the whole thing. You were so over the top that now we have to enjoy the moment a bit. As they say in show business, the heart of all comedy is someone's misfortune. Today, it's yours."

"Yeah, thanks," Craig replied. "As I was saying, I knew there was a significant risk associated with moving that simulator across Norway. My risk management strategy was to plan the route in detail, assess the risk at every turn, and develop a management plan for each possible misadventure. I did all that."

"So what happened?" Dave asked.

Craig took a deep breath as he replied. "I didn't account for the three feet of snow that fell there yesterday. When the flatbed negotiated the last overpass before the air base—the one I had noted as posing an insignificant risk to the transportation effort—the truck was doing 100 kilometers per hour, or about 60 miles per hour. Those three feet of snow on the road raised the flatbed up enough so that when it hit that overpass, it sheered two feet off the crates holding the simulator."

"Whoa!" Dave gasped. "How bad was it?"

"Total loss," Craig replied.

Vince was laughing so hard that his face turned crimson. Dave turned to him with a confused expression on his face. "I'm the new guy here, but I can't imagine how losing a $20 million dollar flight simulator is funny."

Vince gathered his breath, paused a second, and then replied. "Craig is the consummate project risk manager. There is no one I trust more with assessing the risk associated with any part of our flight simulator program. Even so, when he planned this one, he drove us all crazy with his details and calculations."

"So," Vince continued. "When this all happened, we couldn't help but think he was getting his just deserts. That included me, as his boss. It felt like the joke was finally on him."

*Chapter 15* ■ *Risk Management: Even the Best Planning Does Not Eliminate Risk*

"But I destroyed $20 million of equipment," Craig protested. "It's gone. There's nothing I can do about it."

Vince once again clapped Craig on the back. "That's where the joke is on you, old friend. We all appreciate the importance of risk management and the need to assess risks related to any project or any part of a project. Based on your excellent analysis, I had that simulator insured before you shipped it. When anyone is as sure of a plan as you were, I just know something will happen to make that plan go sideways. I insured the simulator well beyond the bonding of the trucking company. I insured it to address the cost of any lost equipment as well as project costs."

Vince continued, "I also insured the project for the potential cost of diverting next month's simulator delivery to Germany to Norway to replace the one we lost, as well as any potential lost profits from the German flight simulator. That last bit will help us refund Germany any liquidated damages for the delay in delivering its simulator. When it all works out in the end, we won't have lost anything at all. Our company will be fine. Our customers will be well taken care of. And we will have had a good laugh about it all."

"Cheer up, man. This is a good day," Vince concluded as he turned and headed back to his office. "It isn't every day that we get one up on the great risk manager himself."

Dave found himself smiling. "I guess, if nothing else, you just proved the benefits of good risk planning."

"Yeah, right," Craig replied. "I think I'll need a beer before I'm likely to agree."

> **Lesson Learned**
>
> *For the project manager and the project sponsor:* Integrate risk management into your projects. There's no predicting every aspect of your project's future.

# Risk Management    16

## Always Follow Up On Your Plans

The sun beat down on the gravel walkways and open grass spaces flanking the long, broad river where the hydroplanes raced. I'd been invited to the Water Follies, a premier hydroplane race and community festival in eastern Washington State by a friend, but I hadn't been prepared for the 95 degree weather, no shade, and races that lasted only a few minutes with hour-long intervals between them. I needed a weekend away from my latest IT project, and heading for the Follies had seemed like a good idea. Now, I was bored, hot, and getting grumpier by the minute.

My host greeted me as I walked past a food booth he and some of his friends were staffing for a charitable cause. "I know just what you need," he said—"one of our famous onion burgers, fries, lemonade, some shade, and company to talk to. I'm buying."

I was solo on this trip across my home state, and wondered about the company. "Who's joining me?"

My friend smiled. "He's another visitor to the area, out of Portland, Oregon. He's a project manager too. I thought you two might hit it off."

He handed me a plastic glass of lemonade and a paper plate full of greasy, good-smelling food and led me to a small picnic table.

A guy a few years younger than me was already sitting there, looking gloomily at his plate.

My friend introduced us. "Gus, this is Dave. He's a project manager too. Thought you two might like to hang out a bit."

Gus got up and shook my hand. "Glad to meet you."

We both sat and dug into our burgers. Starting up the small talk, I commented, "So, you're a project manager too."

"Yep," Gus replied.

"Had any interesting projects lately?" I asked.

Gus sighed. "I guess you could say I've had an interesting project."

"Didn't go so well, I'm guessing. What happened?" I asked.

Gus nodded. "You want to hear the story?"

"Sure," I replied.

"It's kind of ugly," he offered.

I chuckled and replied, "I once had a boss who said he wouldn't hire a project manager who had never failed. He figured someone who had experienced a failed project had learned some good lessons. He was talking about me, just after I nearly tanked a very important project. They had to assign someone to help me to pull my project out of the fire."

"I guess we've all been there," Gus replied.

"If you haven't stumbled, then you've never tried to run across rough ground."

Gus set aside his burger, sipped his drink, and started his story. "I work for the nation's largest telecommunications company. Two years ago, I was assigned to manage a project to replace all the company's switches. It was a major undertaking for

# Chapter 16 ■ Risk Management: Always Follow Up On Your Plans

the company. The switches alone cost over $10 million. The project involved ordering and staging the switches, and then scheduling 10 teams of four technicians to meet the equipment at hundreds of sites around the nation, where they would do the swap-out. There was a bit more technical planning than that involved, but that was the gist of the project."

"I gather that not everything went as planned," I prodded. "What happened?"

"Everything went well at first," Gus replied. "I managed a great purchase effort for the switches, saving the company over 20 percent on the acquisition."

"That doesn't sound so bad," I replied.

"It was great," Gus said. "I was a hero. We budgeted $12 million for the purchase and received the shipment for $10 million—and right on schedule. I managed to have the switches delivered here in September and stored until April, when I would begin staging them for each of the sites across the company. The warehouse was one I'd used many times when working with teams based out of this area. I got a great price on the warehousing and shipping too."

"It sounds like you were doing some great work," I offered.

"I made all the arrangements for storage of the switches while visiting this area to work with my teams. I met the warehouse manager and arranged things in person six months before the equipment was to be shipped to the site. The switches would arrive in numerous large wooden crates. I contracted for covered, indoor storage. The warehouse crew would manage the movement of the crates from the trucks to the warehouse."

"That sounds perfect," I said. "And you said you made a good deal on the price."

"All true," Gus replied. "In fact, the warehouse manager dropped the cost of the labor for locating the crates in the warehouse. I thought it all sounded airtight."

"Ah," I said. "I've had that feeling before myself. You learn to distrust any feelings that suggest things might be going too well in this business."

"You are exactly right; I should have listened to that little voice myself."

"Things took a downturn about the time my team and I were scheduled to come to the warehouse, the following March," Gus continued. "Our goal was to repack the switches and get them shipped to the swap-out sites across the nation. Once the switches were shipped, I would send my teams out to get started on the major effort, the switch upgrades."

"I'm guessing that what you found at the warehouse wasn't what you were hoping for," I speculated.

Gus nodded. "When the equipment was received at the warehouse in October, I confirmed receipt with the warehouse manager by phone from my office in Portland. The inventory he provided matched exactly with the order, so everything seemed to be going according to plan. When he asked if there was anything else he and his warehouse crew could do for me, it never occurred to me that there might have been a misunderstanding and that something was amiss."

"I don't understand," I replied.

"It seems that when the warehouse manager reduced the cost of warehousing by eliminating the cost of the labor to place the crates in the warehouse, he was under the assumption that I would provide a team to complete that task. I thought he was just giving me a price break. What he actually did was remove the requirement for his people to move the crates indoors from the drop site where the delivery company unloaded them."

"So the crates never got moved indoors...." I started.

Gus nodded despairingly. "That's about the size of it."

## Chapter 16 ■ Risk Management: Always Follow Up On Your Plans

"That shouldn't have been so bad," I replied. "The switches were in those big wooden crates."

He cut me off with a raised hand. "Have you ever been in this part of the state between October and March?" I shook my head, no.

"It rains, freezes, snows, thaws, and then freezes, snows, and rains again."

I began to get the picture. "Those wooden crates would not protect much of anything from that sort of harsh weather."

"Exactly," he replied. "When I showed up in March and found the equipment sitting outside, I knew I now had $10 million of worthless junk. The entire shipment was a loss."

"What did you do?"

"What could I do?" he replied. "I reported the situation to my boss, who was the project's sponsor, and ordered the replacement equipment. The expedited replacement shipment cost us an additional $2 million dollars. We arranged to have each switch drop-shipped to the teams' work sites."

"At least you got the equipment to the sites. Did the work get done?" I asked.

Gus nodded again. "Yep. We finished three months late, but we staged the work so that we swapped out the switches in the northern states before winter closed in, and we completed the southern states around the end of fall."

"How did your project sponsor and the company react to all of this?" I asked.

"That's the really odd part of this story," Gus replied. "I had insured the first order when I placed it. As a result, we recovered the full $10 million and applied it to the replacement purchase order. When that came in at $2 million dollars higher than the original order, the final cost for purchasing the switches came

121

out to our original estimate of $12 million. You may recall that I crowed about saving $2 million on that first order."

"So the original estimate for the hardware worked out about right?"

"It did," he replied. "The company had tried to do this same project two years earlier and it had failed miserably. The fact that we got it done at all, even with the delay caused by the reorder, was considered a major success by my project sponsor and the company's president. I got a nice raise and a promotion."

I shook my head slowly and replied, "And so, back to my original question: why so glum? It sounds to me like things worked out pretty well."

"I ruined $10 million of hardware," he replied. "That doesn't feel good."

I met his eyes directly and replied, "I've been in the project management business for a long time. What I recognize in your story is that you identified the importance of that shipment of switches to the project and assessed the risk of any potential loss. You covered that risk by insuring the equipment against loss. That's good risk management in my book."

"In our business," I continued, "stuff happens. No matter how well we plan, no matter how well we consider things, the truth is that you did what any good project manager would do—effective risk management. Your project was delivered a little late, but for a two-year schedule, a slip of three months is only a 12 percent variance. Many of our colleagues would welcome that sort of outcome. The fact that your sponsor and your company gave you a raise and a promotion attests that your efforts were appreciated."

"You make it sound good," Gus said. I noticed the corners of his mouth turn up for the first time.

"You could have managed the storage a bit differently, perhaps by visiting the warehouse once the equipment was received, but that's hindsight at this point. Chalk that one up as a good lesson learned for the future, and accept your victory."

Gus was actually smiling by the time I finished my little speech. "You know, I think you may be right," he said.

"Of course I'm right," I replied. "You know we project managers are never wrong!"

We both laughed and settled back into our little shady spot to share more project management war stories.

> **Lesson Learned**
>
> *For the project manager:* No matter how well you plan, something will generally go awry. Good risk management practices will save the day or at least increase your chances for recovery and a good project outcome.

# PROJECT EXECUTION        17

## Sometimes the Napkin Approach Works

The project manager sat at his desk, fresh from successfully completing a $200,000, six-month technology project. The team of three people he had supervised on the project had done a bang-up job. The client's expressions of gratitude had recently made their way to his consulting firm's management team, and life was looking pretty good.

As his mind slipped off into thoughts of a long, relaxing weekend ahead, his boss came over to his desk and said, in a loud and pleased voice, "Your clients from the project you just completed have asked us to expand the project, to develop the technology further and deploy it throughout their organization. We just received a purchase order for over a million dollars."

The project manager smiled. "I knew they were happy with what we did for them, but a million dollars is a lot of happy."

"You bet it is," his boss replied. "I want you to lead the next phase of this effort. Be in my office in 15 minutes, and bring a copy of the schedule you used for the first phase."

Mark, who had been the project manager's technical lead and software developer for the first project, scooted his chair across the space that separated their cubicles. "Are you going to tell him, or do you want me to?" he whispered.

"Very funny," the project manager replied. "What's to worry about? We followed our standard project methodology in detail. We used discipline and rigor. It was a small project. So I might not have bothered to document it like other people might have..."

"Might not have documented it like a normal project manager? I really would not mind giving him the news," Mark said. "I cannot wait to see his face when he learns the truth."

The project manager gave Mark's chair a solid push, sending the software developer sliding across to his own work space. "At least let me be there when you show him," Mark called. "Not on your life," the project manager replied. "It was my project, and it is my job to tell him."

The project manager reached into his top desk drawer and retrieved a tattered and worn napkin. Napkin in hand, he walked over to his boss' office.

Excitedly, his boss told greeted him with "I have more good news. We just got word that your team's project was nominated for the state's best website project. The judging has been completed and you all took second place. On top of that, your project took first place in the same category in the southwest region. You were competing against projects as much as 10 times larger. Congratulations!"

They shook hands, and his boss then asked, "Did you bring your schedule with you? I thought we might use it as a starting point for scoping the next phase for your clients."

"I did," the project manager replied. Hesitantly, he laid the napkin on his boss' desk, spreading it out so that the notes on it were plainly visible. In several places, the napkin was so worn that it had split. Many of the words on it had been smudged.

"What's this?" his boss asked.

"It's the schedule," the project manager replied. He watched as his boss' face began to color.

# Chapter 17 ■ Project Execution: Sometimes the Napkin Approach Works

"Do you mean to tell me that you successfully delivered an award-winning technology project, which our clients love, which our clients have now offered us a million dollars to expand, on a napkin?"

The project manager wondered if his days as a project management consultant had just come to an inglorious end. "That's about the size of it, sir."

His boss sat and stared at the napkin for several minutes before rising from his chair. "Don't move," he said. "I want someone else to see this."

A few minutes later, the project manager's boss returned with the consulting firm's president in tow. The boss pointed to the napkin. "There it is," he said.

The project manager held his breath as the company president leaned over the napkin and appeared to study it carefully. The president stepped back from the napkin, turned to the project manager's boss and considered him for several long moments before turning back to the project manager and sticking out his hand. "Congratulations," he said.

The project manager stood and shook the president's hand. "Thanks, sir."

"You did a fine job on that project," the company president said. "You will be seeing a nice bonus in your next paycheck. And so will your team members."

"But what about the napkin?" his boss stammered. "Have you ever seen anything so...."

The company president cut off the boss' words. "You can't argue with results. In this case, the napkin approach worked. The awards...the new contract for a million dollars...you just can't argue with that."

The president turned to the project manager. "You keep this up and you'll be a principal in the firm in no time. Thank you, gentlemen," he said as he turned away.

"I guess that means I'm not fired?" the project manager asked.

"Not by a long shot," his boss replied. "However, we are going to get you some training with an automated project scheduling tool."

The project manager readily agreed. "I think that might be a good idea."

> **Lessons Learned**
>
> *For the project manager:* It's the project outcome that matters when all is said and done. For large projects, execute a well-documented project plan and schedule. For small efforts, focus on getting the project done rather than on developing extensive plans.
>
> *For the project sponsor:* You can't argue with good results. It's the project outcome that matters.

# HUMAN RESOURCE MANAGEMENT 18

## Know Your Team

A lesson learned at someone else's expense is a lesson learned the hard way.

Joe was a great guy. His small project team of six was crazy about him. On projects, Joe assumed the role of quiet listener and competent, if hesitant, contributor at project team meetings; he unfailingly made time for anyone who needed an ear.

As the new information technology project for a major state agency geared up, the project manager for the job, who was relatively new to the software integration firm, jumped at the chance to select Joe for his team. The project manager's enthusiasm was kindled by the recommendations of the team's technical lead, who praised all aspects of Joe's life and character, not to mention Joe's impressive resume of software development projects.

Excitement filled the room on the day of project kick-off, as the technical lead handed out assignments. Database model construction landed in one team member's lap. The security model for the web-based application to be constructed went to another person. Business analysis responsibilities migrated to the business team, led by the project manager, who would do double duty in that capacity. The technical lead held tasks related to solution architecture, code development, and configuration management for himself and a few others, including Joe.

When the project manager and the technical lead met later in the day to review the project team's assignments, Joe's name came up. The technical lead noted that Joe would be developing the logon screen for the project. Logon screens are simple to develop, as they are generally cut and pasted from one software application to another with little modification.

Satisfied that the technical lead had doled out the assignments appropriately, the project manager left the meeting and got started on his own work.

A week later, the project team met for a brief review of the project's risks, issues, and overall progress. Near the end of the meeting, the project manager and technical lead worked their way down the list of assignments, noting each team member's accomplishments over the past week, their plans for the following week, and any roadblocks they had encountered. The business analysts reported experiencing some difficulty with the new method of documenting system requirements, but otherwise the reports were overwhelmingly positive.

When the discussion reached Joe, the technical lead looked in his direction. Joe nodded his head in response, mumbling something so quietly that no one could make out what he said. The technical lead and project manager took that as a good sign and proceeded with the meeting's agenda.

Another week passed, and the project team gathered again. Once again, progress reports yielded largely favorable results, although the business analysts were working overtime to keep up, having little experience with the new capability-mapping approach to documenting business requirements.

Joe, however, was not present. Another member of the team mentioned that Joe was not feeling well and was not at work that day. No one commented on Joe's progress on the logon screen, immersed as they were in their own work. Everyone, including the project manager and technical lead, knew that Joe's assignment was one of the easiest on the project's task list;

they therefore assumed that all was well. The meeting adjourned and all returned to work feeling good about their progress.

Events conspired to preclude a project team meeting the following week, and so it wasn't until two weeks later that the team gathered again to review the project's progress. The team was working on a tight timeline, with several key deliverables looming on the horizon. All were eager to check off their assignments as complete, and with few exceptions did so. One of those exceptions was Joe.

When the conversation came around to Joe, he shook his head sadly and replied to the question about his progress. "I've had some difficulties with the logon page. I can't seem to get it to work at all."

"But I thought that was a pretty straightforward task," the project manager replied.

"Let me meet with Joe after the meeting," the technical lead offered. "I'm sure we can work things out. I'll get back to you later this afternoon."

Near the end of the day the technical lead entered the project manager's office. "I met with Joe an hour ago," she started.

"And...?" the project manager prompted.

"He hadn't made any progress at all, so I worked with him for 45 minutes. In that time, we copied and pasted a logon page with the background code and put it into place in the test version of the new software."

"That's good, then," the project manager replied.

"Not really," said the technical lead. "I did all the work myself—and did what it has taken Joe a month to not accomplish, in 45 minutes. Joe watched and appeared a little lost through the process."

"But his resume says he's a software developer," the project manager replied. "You all indicated that the logon screen was a simple task that anyone could handle. It should have been a cinch for someone like Joe. He's got what, six projects under his belt over the past five years?"

"Joe's experience was with another branch of our company, in another state," the technical lead replied. "I accepted his experience based on his resume and the fact that he was an intra-company transfer. I concluded he would be right for this project and specifically his current assignment. But clearly we have a problem with Joe and I'm not sure what to do about it."

The project manager looked at his watch and suggested, "Let's sleep on it tonight. We'll figure out what to do about this situation in the morning."

A few minutes after the technical lead left the project manager's office, the project manager's boss showed up at the door. He greeted the project manager and pulled up a chair. "How are things?" he asked cheerfully.

The project manager set aside his briefcase and replied, "For the most part, very good. I do have one situation that I could use some advice about."

"Shoot," his boss replied.

"As you know, I retired from the military several years ago. In the military, I served as a troubleshooter, going to installations and military bases where the government determined that something needed to be cleaned up. I normally got the tough assignments, although that experience made me, I believe, a good project manager and prepared to tackle any task. On the other hand, quite a number of people ended up being displaced or losing their jobs as a result of those cleanup jobs. Not that they didn't deserve it, but it weighed on me."

"I recall our discussions about that when you started here," his boss replied.

"Then you also recall that I specifically requested, as a condition of employment, that I not be in a position to fire anyone in the future."

"I do," his boss replied. "Are you having a problem with one of your team members?"

The project manager nodded. "I am. He's a great guy and the team loves him, but he's having some difficulty with a very basic task that makes me wonder if he has the software development skills we need for this project."

"You're talking about Joe, I assume," said the boss. The project manager nodded. "Don't worry, then. I can handle this situation," his boss replied.

"I don't want to fire him," the project manager added. His boss nodded, stood up, and left the office.

The next morning, the project team gathered for a special progress review. They had a meeting with the client scheduled for later in the day and wanted to review the script for demonstrating the new software system's functionality.

Joe was absent. The technical lead was noticeably upset. The project manager pulled her aside. "Where's Joe?" he asked.

"He was let go this morning, when he arrived for work. He's gone," she said.

"What?" the project manager demanded, stalking out of the conference room before the technical lead could reply. A few minutes later, he was in his boss' office, demanding to know what had happened to Joe.

"Joe had two strikes against him when he arrived here, before we put him on your project. The issue of the logon page was his third strike. He's out," the boss replied.

"Why didn't I know about those two strikes, and the nature of them, when he was put on our team?" the project manager demanded. "I as good as had him fired as a result of asking you for advice about handling the situation."

"It's not our policy to dredge up past offenses when we transfer a person to a team. And I'm sorry you feel that way about how this went down. I thought by my letting Joe go, you would not have to carry the blame and ill feelings."

"Well, you figured wrong," the project manager replied.

"I'm sorry to hear that," his boss said as the project manager retreated from the office.

Two months later, after successfully meeting a significant project milestone, the project team went to lunch at a local restaurant. The project manager's anger over Joe's being let go and his boss' decision not to tell him about Joe's past had abated somewhat, but still lingered.

Over burgers and fries, one of the software developers commented, "I heard from Joe yesterday."

The project manager perked up and asked, "How's he doing?"

"Great," the software developer said. "He landed another job only a week after he left our team. He's a requirements manager for one of our competitors. Seems what he lacked in software skills, he made up for in people skills and the ability to interpret business needs into technical requirements."

The technical lead was quick to add, "I heard from him as well. He's very happy in his job. Looks like he found his niche."

The technical lead paused and then directed her words toward the project manager. "We could have used those skills a month ago when you all were having such a hard time documenting the business requirements for our project."

"We sure could have," the project manager replied. "If only I'd known he had those skills."

> **Lesson Learned**
>
> *For the project manager:* Know your team members. Know them well. No matter what tools might be used to manage a project, it is the human resource that ultimately gets the work done. Match the right person to the right job, or live with the consequences in terms of project impact as well as potential personal and professional costs.

# PROJECT MANAGEMENT INTEGRATION                              19

## Solution Complexity Is Seldom the Issue

For the past 15 years, the project manager's career had focused on saving projects that were on the skids, bringing them from the edge of failure to successful completion. Organizations approached him on a monthly and even weekly basis, requesting his services to pull one project or another out of the fire; there were that many challenged projects in the large metropolitan area where he lived and worked.

This project manager didn't consider himself unusually intelligent or skilled at project management. In fact, his professional self-image might have surprised people. Complexities that others commonly dwelled on when it came to technology, training, or business process engineering efforts generally eluded him as he plugged through basic project management processes to do his job.

Another cold, September day drew to a close as the project manager gathered his laptop computer, project files, and a very few mementoes, preparing to close his office of the last two years. This most recent project had been challenging, but it was now complete and it was time to move on to something new. His thoughts drifted back over the long haul of the project, lingering only briefly on its challenges when his cell phone buzzed.

"Good morning, Bill," the caller said, asking if Bill might be willing to meet with him that afternoon to discuss a project at his company that was not going well.

Bill glanced at his watch. 4:00 pm. The caller's office was just down the road, so he agreed to meet for coffee in a half hour.

An efficient administrative assistant greeted Bill at the front door of the company's office building. She escorted him to the top floor, where the CEO of the firm greeted Bill enthusiastically.

"We need you, Bill," he started. "I understand that you specialize in helping companies like ours when our projects get in trouble."

Bill nodded. "It seems like that has been my career for the past decade or so, although it wasn't by design. What can I do for you?"

The CEO smiled, but his look was apologetic. "I have to warn you that this project is way more complex than those you might have encountered in the past. It involves re-engineering our business processes, automating them, and then getting the new system and processes in place in time for us to compete successfully for a very large business opportunity. We have already wasted six months of the potential schedule and have a year left to get the project done. So far, no one has been able to line up all the parts successfully. We have had false starts, user rejection, stakeholder infighting, and surprises all along the way."

"Your situation is not all that uncommon," Bill replied.

"Do you think you can help us?" the CEO asked.

Bill nodded. "I'll need some more details, but it sounds like situations I have dealt with before. I could stop by tomorrow morning and look at the information you've gathered for the project. If I don't take the project or you don't like my approach, we can shake hands and I'll walk away. If we agree that I can

*Chapter 19 ■ Project Management Integration: Solution Complexity Is Seldom the Issue*

help get your project back on track, we can talk terms for a contract then."

The CEO stood up and shook Bill's hand. "I'll look forward to hearing what you have to say tomorrow over lunch."

The next morning, Bill was at work early. He spent three hours poring over well-organized project files that included a project charter outlining the budget, timelines, and the business problem the company was attempting to resolve. Essentially, the company was seeking to establish itself as a provider of unique investment services.

Bill noted that someone on the project team had done an excellent job of documenting individual stakeholder needs and detailed business requirements. The requirements were organized in a manner that Bill anticipated would serve the team well when it came time to build the IT system to support the new business process. The rest of the files included hundreds of emails, draft schedules, and letters from interested investors. As organized as the files were, however, they lacked most of the project artifacts.

Bill met the CEO for lunch the next day. The CEO was eager to know if Bill thought he could help with the project.

Bill nodded. "After this initial review, I believe I can get this project done for you in the coming year, provided the resources are made available to build an effective project team and the budget is there."

"This is a high-priority project for this firm," the CEO replied. "Whatever you need, I will get for you. What, exactly, do you think you'll need to do to get the project on track?"

"It's pretty straightforward, I think," Bill said. "You have good stakeholder information, a good problem statement, and some excellent business requirements. With some basic project organization, planning, and controlled execution, we should have this project done without a lot of fuss."

The CEO frowned. "My top people have worked on this project for six months. They assured me that it was the complexity of the task that made things so difficult. I believe them, so I'm surprised to hear you suggest otherwise."

"It's my experience that it is seldom the complexity of the business case that challenges an organization's ability to deliver a project successfully. Those not experienced with project management processes generally see complexity as an issue. In my world, complexity relates simply to the number of tasks that need to be done to deliver the required product, service, or result, and that's simply a matter of breaking down the requirements to the level necessary to understand the work. Your team has already done that, so completing this project should be pretty straightforward, as long as we use a good, disciplined project management approach."

"I'm not saying that the work won't be arduous," Bill continued. "What you plan to accomplish is challenging. What I am saying is that setting the project up in a manner that allows your company to deliver what you need is a relatively simple matter."

The CEO extended his hand to Bill. "I appreciate your time today. I really do. But I cannot accept your conclusion that this project, which has stymied my team for six months, can be accomplished so easily. I've seen too much frustration and difficulty to accept that."

"No problem," replied Bill. "I was glad to come over and take a look."

Bill turned to leave, but then paused and turned back to the CEO. "Just one thing before I leave: In all the years I have been doing project management, and specifically, working with floundering projects like yours, I have never once encountered a project that was failing because of the complexity of the business problem or technology. It has always been a matter of organizing the project well and implementing solid initiation, planning, management and control, risk management, scope management, and all those other key project management processes. Those are the things that save projects, and those

*Chapter 19 ■ Project Management Integration: Solution Complexity Is Seldom the Issue*

are the same things that can save yours. I wish you the best of luck."

Bill took the next three weeks off, recuperating from his recent efforts and researching new business opportunities. Late into the third week, the CEO he'd talked to about the failed project called him.

"Good afternoon, Bill. Do you think we might get together once more to discuss the project we have had so much difficulty with over the past seven months?"

"I'm not sure what more I can offer," Bill replied. "Your project is eminently doable, and I described to you how I would go about getting it done. Has something changed?"

"No, not really," the CEO replied. "We have burned another month or so of effort and made little progress. I hired a very expensive project manager, who was here for two weeks before throwing up her hands and quitting. I'm at my wit's end, and the board is pressuring me for some positive, visible signs of progress. Would you be willing to come in and take a shot at the project?"

Bill sighed. "I don't have anything more interesting on my plate right now, and I believe your project can be successful. If you agree to let me run the project as I believe it needs to be run, then I'll take the job."

"Whatever you need," the CEO replied.

The next week, Bill went to work on the project. As complex as the business problem was, he tackled the project as he would any other effort. He asked for and received two business analysts to help him refine the project's vision and objectives. He developed a project charter that the CEO signed, commenting as he did so that the document provided clarity that hadn't been evident on the project before.

Once the project was chartered, Bill engaged his business team's subject matter experts in the task of refining the requirements that had been developed earlier. They then began the somewhat tedious task of identifying the work needed to deliver those requirements. New members were added to the team who possessed the skill sets to define the work in detail and plan how it might be done. When that effort was completed, a solid project team had been constructed, along with a detailed project schedule and a list of risks associated with the work plan.

A month later, the project was in full swing. Business processes were defined and documented. Technical and functional designs were completed for the new IT system. A training program was developed to train the organization's employees in how to use the new system and leverage the new business processes to position the firm for entry into the new business market. Ten months later—one month ahead of schedule—the project was complete, the employees of the organization were ready to move forward, and the CEO was beaming.

At the project close party held shortly after launching the new IT system, everyone gathered to celebrate the project's success. The CEO walked up and presented each member of the team, who were laughing and sharing stories of the project's success, with a nice bonus check. "I can't thank you all enough," he said.

The CEO then turned to Bill. "And I can't thank you enough, ever. When you told me this project was a straightforward effort that could be delivered using basic project management processes, I was lost in the complexity of the business I saw driving the project. I am so grateful you got my head out of those clouds and my feet firmly on the ground. It is a lesson I am not likely to forget."

"You are welcome," Bill replied. He turned to the rest of the team. "For all of you, remember that it is seldom the perceived complexity of a project's goals or objectives that drives success or failure. Success comes from following good project management processes. Success always comes down to the basics of initiating, planning, and executing a project and paying attention to

Chapter 19 ■ *Project Management Integration: Solution Complexity Is Seldom the Issue*

the key knowledge areas, including scope management, risk management, and project team management."

"Yeah," replied one of the team's business team leaders. "But you only mentioned project initiation, planning, and execution. What about project closeout? What about the party you have at project close, like we're having right now?"

Everyone cheered as the CEO beamed. "Let's hear it for the party and our success!"

> **Lesson Learned**
>
> *For the project sponsor:* The perceived complexity of a project's solution is seldom the driver of project success or failure. Success is driven by adherence to basic project management processes, integrated to deliver an effective solution. Although the work can be lengthy and arduous, the process is always simple and straightforward.